Brothers In War

Nabbe Brothers in World War II

Robert William Nabbe
with Melissa Nabbe Matusevich

Brothers In War

Nabbe Brothers in World War II

Robert William Nabbe
with Melissa Nabbe Matusevich

Book design by Michael Abraham

ISBN 10: 0-926487-74-4
ISBN 13: 978-0-926487-74-1

Printed in the United States of America

Pocahontas Press
www.pocahontaspress.com

PREFACE

When I was a little girl I often heard my father talk about his experiences as a soldier during the Second World War. His was different from most; Dad was stationed in the Washington, D.C. area where he served as a chauffeur for officers. At times I would ask him to tell me, once again, the story about the dead colonel or to describe the time he sat in President Roosevelt's chair and put his feet up on the desk. Dad always complied, regaling me with stories of his service in the Motor Pool in the Military District of Washington.

As an adult I came to understand that history is the story of people, all people. Certainly General Eisenhower deserves to be remembered, but so does the private who chauffeured Eisenhower while he was on official business in our nation's capital. With this in mind I began to nag my father to write down what he remembered of his army days. Years passed and I feared the stories would be forgotten as they dimmed with time. Eventually, I suggested to Dad that he tape his memories, and I promised to transfer his oral history to written form. So, late in life my father, with a surprisingly vivid memory, recorded his memoir and gave it to me to transcribe.

Sometime after the transcription was complete, I took possession of the letters Dad's brother sent to him from the front lines of World War II. I was immediately struck by the vast difference in the war experiences of two brothers close in age and closer in bond. While one remained stateside chauffeuring generals in Washington, the other stormed the beach on D-Day and fought the Germans in the Battle of the Bulge. The contrast between the two experiences could not have been greater.

The letters were so fragile that it became necessary to transcribe them as well. When that task was complete, I asked Dad to read through the letters to explain various points that I did not understand. For clarification I added Dad's comments as footnotes at the bottom of the letters. In this book the transcriptions retain the original spellings and punctuation as Richard wrote them.

This book weaves together the story of two brothers who served in the United States Army during World War II: Pfc. Robert William Nabbe whose service in Washington was vastly different from most and Cpl. Richard Frederick Nabbe whose letters portray both the horrors of war along with the mundane experiences of soldiers in battle.

Melissa Nabbe Matusevich

ACKNOWLEDGEMENTS

Special thanks to Jane Abraham, Brenda Wojciechowski, Melanie Harvey, and Paul Mather whose help was invaluable in bringing this project to fruition.

INTRODUCTION

Most stories of military experience deal with the horror and heroics of war. I heard it implied that during World War II in the U.S. Army there were approximately seven support troops for every rifleman actually engaged in combat. I am one of those seven soldiers who did not confront a hostile enemy and who, by the grace of the gods of war, spent thirty-eight months in uniform in a safe environment doing my duty for our country.

Every serviceman knows he cannot select or choose his place in a vast war machine. You go where you are assigned at the pleasure of the War Department. Fortunately for me, the War Department needed drivers in their huge motor pool in the Military District of Washington, and that is where I was sent to drive general officers after training in Fort Dix, New Jersey. My story attempts to tell the experiences of one of those support troops established at a safe post far from the perils of war that our country was engaged in around the globe.

Robert W. Nabbe

To you who answered the call of your country and served in its Armed Forces to bring about the total defeat of the enemy, I extend the heartfelt thanks of a grateful Nation. As one of the Nation's finest, you undertook the most severe task one can be called upon to perform. Because you demonstrated the fortitude, resourcefulness and calm judgment necessary to carry out that task, we now look to you for leadership and example in further exalting our country in peace.

Harry Truman

THE WHITE HOUSE

ROBERT WILLIAM NABBE

RICHARD FREDERICK NABBE

Brothers In War

Nabbe Brothers in World War II

DRAFTED

My first exposure to the military occurred before December 7, 1941, the day of the Japanese attack on Pearl Harbor. The United States had been tentatively, but I wouldn't say secretly, preparing for war because I was drafted for a period of one year somewhere about the beginning of June 1941. I was taken to Fort Dix, New Jersey and went through a series of tests and physicals. At that point in time, the Army decided that my vision was just a little bit less than what they required. They ultimately lowered their requirements to where people almost ready for a white cane could get into the military.

I was sent back home and put on reserve status. Later in the same year, 1941, December 7, the attack on Pearl Harbor occurred. I heard the news on the radio, as did most everybody else in the country. We didn't have television then. The world just stopped for everybody at that moment—at least everybody in the United States. I was with a friend of mine, Joe Urban. At that point, we realized that our age of innocence was over. I guess I was around twenty-one or twenty-two. I knew that it would be only a matter of time before I would be in the military.

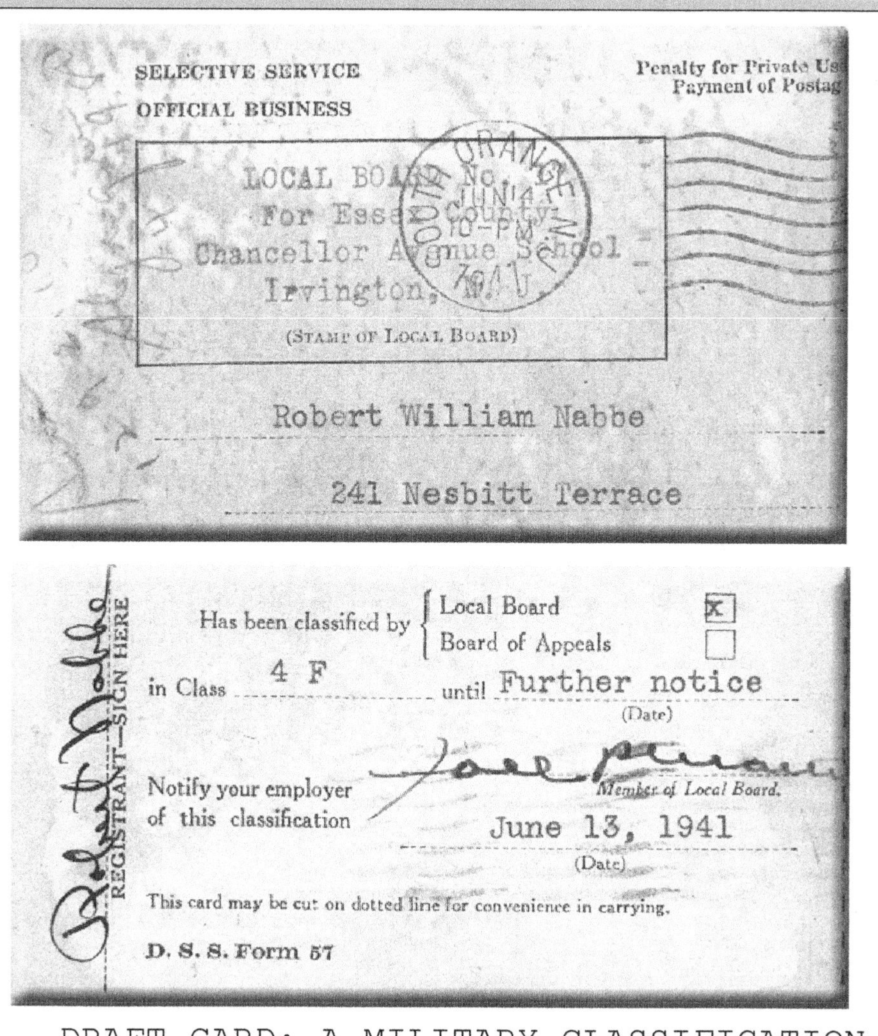

DRAFT CARD: A MILITARY CLASSIFICATION
OF 4 F INDICATED THAT THE DRAFTEE WAS
UNFIT FOR SERVICE DUE TO A PHYSICAL OR
MENTAL DISABILITY. ROBERT'S EYESIGHT,
FROM AN EARLY AGE, WAS WEAK. NEARSIGHT-
ED, HE RECEIVED HIS FIRST PAIR OF COR-
RECTIVE LENSES AT AGE FOUR. IN 1941 HIS
VISION IN EACH EYE WAS 20/400 FAR FROM
20/20, WHICH IS NORMAL.

Prepare in Triplicate

LOCAL BOARD No. 17
For Essex County
Chancellor Avenue School
Irvington, N. J.
(STAMP OF LOCAL BOARD)

May 31, 1941
(Date of mailing)

ORDER TO REPORT FOR INDUCTION

The President of the United States,

To   Robert   William   Nabbe
       (First name)   (Middle name)   (Last name)

Order No.   746

GREETING:

Having submitted yourself to a Local Board composed of your neighbors for the purpose of determining your availability for training and service in the armed forces of the United States, you are hereby

notified that you have now been selected for training and service in the   Army
                                                           (Army, Navy, Marine Corps)

You will, therefore, report to the Local Board named above at   Chancellor Avenue School
Irvington, New Jersey
                                             (Place of reporting)

at   7:00   A. m., on the   11th   day of   June   , 19 41.
(Hour of reporting)

This Local Board will furnish transportation to an induction station of the service for which you have been selected. You will there be examined and if accepted for training and service, you will then be inducted into the stated branch of the service.

If you are not accepted, you will be furnished transportation to the place where you reported. Wilful failure to report promptly to this Local Board at the hour and on the day named in this notice is a violation of the Selective Training and Service Act of 1940 and subjects the violator to fine and imprisonment. Bring with you sufficient clothing for 3 days.

You must keep this form and take it with you when you report to your Local Board.

Joel A. Martin
(Signature)
                           Member of Local Board.

D. S. S. Form 150

The following will be completed by the officer in charge of the induction station examining the selected man, and one copy returned by mail to the Local Board named:

June 11, 1941
(Date)

STRIKE INAPPLICABLE SECTION:

1. Accepted for service in
(Army, Navy, Marine Corps)

2. Rejected for training and service and instructed to return to Local Board named in this order for

the following cause: Vision Defective, Bilateral

NOTE.—If rejected for physical disqualification, the duplicate of physical examination made at induction station must be attached.

Officer in Charge of Induction Station.
John Scially
Major Inf.
Commanding Officer

The original of this form to be mailed to the selected man, and the other two copies to be attached to Form 151 and forwarded to the induction station with the men ordered to report.

To be prepared in TRIPLICATE

REJECTED SELECTEE

**REPORT OF INDUCTION OF
SELECTIVE SERVICE MAN**

Do not enter anything in this column

Residence	
State	County

(Last name)   (First name)   (Middle name)   (Army serial No.)

Permanent address ______ (Town) ______ (County) ______ (State) † ______ {Urban ☐ / Rural ☐} ______ (Mother tongue)

Place inducted

Birthplace ______ (City, town, or county) ______ (State or country) ______ Birth date ______ (Month) ‡ (Day) (Year)

Date inducted

Day	Month	Year

Age: ______ years ______ months. U. S. citizen ______ (Yes or No)   Race ______

If an applicant for citizenship, show date and court in which application was made: ______

Source	Nativity

If not a citizen, show country of allegiance: ______

Grade completed in grammar school: ______ ; high school: ______ ; college or university: ______

Year of birth

Civilian trade or occupation: ______ ; years so engaged: ______ ; weekly wage: ______

Marital status: ______ (Single, married, widower, or divorced)   Dependents: ______ (State number and relationship)

Race/Cit.	Education

Previous service in United States military or naval service, Marine Corps, Coast Guard, or National Guard in an active, inactive, or reserve status: ______ (State last service only)

Occupation	Marital

† Place "X" in box opposite urban if community of 2,500 population or greater; otherwise place "X" in box opposite rural.

NEAREST RELATIVE AND PERSON TO BE NOTIFIED IN CASE OF EMERGENCY

Nearest relative ______ (Other than wife or minor child) ______ (Name in full)

Relationship ______ Mother ______ Address ______ (Number and street or rural route; if none, so state) ______ (City, town, or post office) ______ (State or country)

Person to be notified in case of emergency ______ (Name in full)

Relationship ______ (If friend, so state) ______ Address ______ (Number and street or rural route; if none, so state) ______ (City, town, or post office) ______ (State or country)

DESIGNATION OF BENEFICIARY

The persons eligible to be my beneficiary are designated below:

1. ______ (Full name of wife; if no wife, or if she is deceased or divorced, so state) ______ (Wife's full address)

2. ______ (Full name and address of each minor child, and each dependent child over 21 years of age. If there are no children, so state. If the address is the same as the wife's, so state. Do not repeat address)

In the event of my leaving no widow or child, or their decease before payment is made, I then designate as my beneficiary the relative whose name, relationship, and address are shown below:

3. ______ (If designation is beneficiary is relative that must state in own handwriting "I declare to be alternate beneficiary")

In the event of the death or disqualification of the last-named dependent relative before payment is made, I then designate as my beneficiary the relative whose name, relationship, and address are shown below:

4. ______ (If beneficiary is named in line 3 but naming of alternate is declined, man must state in own handwriting: "I decline to designate an alternate beneficiary.")

The above recorded information is correct.

Signature of inducted man: ______ (First name) ______ (Middle initial) ______ (Last name)

Witnessed at ______ TRENTON, N. J. ______ on ______ JUN 11 1941 ______ 19___

JOHN W. LEARY 2nd Lt Inf

PHYSICAL EXAMINATION

1. Eye abnormalities .... Insufficient Vision Blepharitis

2. Ear, nose, throat abnormalities .... None

3. Mouth and gum abnormalities .... None

Right	(Examinee's)	Left

4. Teeth { 8 7 ~~6~~ 5 4 3 2 1   1 2 3 4 5 6 7 8   (Strike out those that are missing; circle those that
      { 16 15 14 ~~13~~ 12 11 10 9   9 10 11 12 13 ~~14~~ 15 16   may be restored)

5. Skin .... Normal

6. Varicose veins .... None

7. Hernia .... None

8. Hemorrhoids .... None

9. Genitalia .... Normal

10. Feet .... Normal

11. Musculo-skeletal defects .... Normal

12. Abdominal viscera .... Normal

13. Cardiovascular system .... Normal

14. Lungs, including X-ray, if made .... Increased bronchial markings

15. Nervous system: reflexes, pupillary .... Normal   patellar .... Sluggish

16. Endocrine disturbances .... Negative

17. Results of laboratory examinations, when made ....

18. Remarks on defects not sufficiently described above ....

19. Summary of defects in order of importance, impression of physical fitness ....
     Nervous & Mental   Negative
     Build   Medium
     Scars & Marks   None

Vision:
Right eye 20/ 400   20/20-
Left eye 20/ 400   20/20-

Hearing:
Right ear .... 20 / 20
Left ear .... 20 / 20

Height .... 69 .... in.

Weight .... 172 .... lb.

Girth (at nipples):
Inspiration .... 39 .... in.
Expiration .... 37 .... in.

Girth (at umbilicus) .... 34½ in.

Posture .... Good

Frame .... Large

Color of hair .... Blonde

Color of eyes .... Hazle

Complexion .... Ruddy

Pulse:*
Sitting 92
After exercise ....
2 min. after exercise ....

Blood pressure:*
Systolic 130
Diastolic 86

Urinalysis:
Sp. gr. .... Ina.
Albumin .... Negative
Sugar .... Negative
Microscopic* .... Negative
Other data* ....

*When required.

I certify that the above-named registrant was carefully examined; that the results of the examination have been correctly recorded and that to the best of my knowledge and belief he is—
*Mentally and physically qualified for the active military service of the United States.
*Mentally physically disqualified for the military service of the United States by reason of .... Vision Defective, Bilateral
*Physically qualified only for limited service in the Army of the United States by reason of ....

Place .... TRENTON, N. J.   Signature ....

Date .... JUN 11 1941   Name typed or stamped: .... W F Guidotti Capt M C .... Medical Corps,
          (Grade)

I acknowledge receipt of copy of this report this date .... JUN 11 1941
          (Date)   (Signature of inducted or rejected man. Required only on original)

The above-named registrant was this date—
*Accepted for active military service limited service and inducted into the Army of the United States and sent to ....
          (Post, camp, or reception center)

*Rejected for service in the Army of the United States.

Place .... TRENTON, N. J. ....
          (Signature of inducting officer)

Date .... JUN 11 1941 .... JOHN W LEARY 2nd Lt Inf.
          (Typed name of inducting officer) (Grade and organization)

*# Strike out clause or words not applicable.

FINGERPRINTS—RIGHT HAND

WAR DEPARTMENT
THE ADJUTANT GENERAL'S OFFICE
WASHINGTON, D. C.

———

OFFICIAL BUSINESS

PENALTY FOR PRIVATE USE TO AVOID
PAYMENT OF POSTAGE, $300

Mrs. Edna Mae Nabbe
241 Nesbit Terrace
Irvington, New Jersey

TRENTON, N. J.   JUN 11 1941
———————————   ———————————
(Induction Station)   (Date)

This is to advise you that

ROBERT WILLLAM NABBE ________________________________ has been
(Name)   (Army Serial No., if accepted)

____
(Reception Center, Replacement Center, or other installation)

at ____
(Post Office address)

*rejected for active military service and returned to his home.

This card to be made out and mailed at Induction Station at time of transfer therefrom.
*Strike out clause not applicable.

W. D., A. G. O. Form No. 202
March 15, 1941

16—18394   U. S. GOVERNMENT PRINTING OFFICE

ENTERING SERVICE

Rather than wait to be drafted again, I decided I'd enlist in the Navy. I'd rather have been in the Navy than the Army at that time. I went down to Newark to the Navy recruiting center and explained that I had less than the level of vision required for the Army. The Navy doctors, however, said that my vision was just perfect for their purposes. I didn't have to have 20/20 vision without glasses. They were quite interested in signing me up. I told the recruiter that I'd already been drafted, at one time, into the Army branch of the military. When the Navy began checking, they found out that the Army still had a hold on me and wouldn't release me. Ultimately, I wound up going back into the Army.

Of course, I didn't go into the Army right away. I went back to the job I had with Weston Electric Instrument Company in Newark, New Jersey where they were making all kinds of war materials for Great Britain as well as for our own armed forces. By the time December 10th, 1942 came around, the Army recalled me. This time I left on December 17th, just prior to Christmas. It was a pretty unhappy time for me to have to leave the family just before Christmas day. I wound up in Fort Dix, New Jersey along with a gazillion other guys just like myself—miserable, unhappy and torn up from our home roots, not knowing what the future held for us.

Fort Dix, at that point in the war, was not fully equipped to receive hundreds and hundreds of inductees. We were herded around in huge masses and finally wound up established in a kind of tent city. I believe there were eight men to a tent. We had a little conical type of stove in the center, a little sheet metal thing that you threw coal into. It was one of those situations where those who were closest to the stove were warm throughout the cold winter nights. Those of us along the outside walls of the tent nearly froze in our cots.

Of course we didn't have a lot of time in the tent to get cold because they kept us pretty busy. There were all kinds of training programs that we had to undergo and then there was the inevitable kitchen police (KP) that I got stuck with a couple of times. There were also the work details.

AUTHORIZATION FOR ALLOTMENT OF PAY
(See AR 35-5520)

Send directly to Chief of Finance, Allotment Division
Bldg. X, 19th & B Sts., NE, Washington, D. C.

Nabbe,	Robert	W.	82598454	Pvt	1229th R C
(Last Name)	(First Name)	(Middle Initial)	(Army serial No.)	(Grade)	(Company, regiment, or arm or service)

National Service Life Insurance   6.60

The { *officer* / *enlisted man* } named above hereby authorizes a Class N allotment of his pay in the amount of $__________ per month for the period of __XXX__ months, commencing __December__ 19_42_ and expiring ___E T S___ , 19___

2 deductions will be made from first pay of applicant.

to __Veterans Administration______________________________ Washington, D. C._______
  (Name of allottee)   (Code No.)   (Number and street of rural route)   (City, town, or post office)   (State)

Date of enlistment   Dec 17 ______________________, 19___ When other than "Pay of the Army" is affected, state P.A.

chargeable ______ X X X X X X X X X X X X

I hereby state that the purpose for which this allotment is granted is solely for the support of wife, child, or dependent relatives; or if made for the payment of life insurance premiums, the insurance (including endowments and/or twenty (or other) payment policies) is on the life of the allotter only; that a policy therefor has been issued and the first premium paid thereon; that the insurance constitutes the major and not a merely incidental or collateral element of the transaction; and that the allotment is made in favor of the insurance company issuing the policy and not in favor of a bank or other agent. I also state if allotment is in favor of a bank that deposit should be made to the credit of

_____ X X X X X X _______________ X X X X X X _____
        (Name)   (Relationship)

X _Robert W. Nabbe_______
        (Signature of allotter)

Place ___1229th A C   Fort Dix N J ___   Date   Dec 19 ______________, 19_42_

Entered on service record.   Dec 19 1942

AUTHORIZATION FOR ALLOTMENT OF PAY

EARLY ARMY LIFE

One work detail in particular that I remember was being on the coal truck. At the end of every company street was a huge box that was kept full of coal. That's where we drew the coal for the individual tents. It was our job to load the coal onto this big truck and to bring it back and fill all of the coal boxes. By the time we got the last one filled, the first one was already empty, so we went back and did all of that over again.

I remember one time when we were going back to the coal dump. There was a truck coming toward us on a narrow little road. Another vehicle, which was ahead of us, was down below the rise of a hill. And as they came up over the top of the hill, for some reason, the two drivers met head on. There were Colored soldiers in the coal truck that got hit. When the two trucks collided, those men who were in the bed of the truck—as well as all that coal—came flying out in one huge sheet. It was just incredible that nobody was really seriously hurt. I'll never forget that.

There were thousands of troops in training in Fort Dix, and everybody was dressed alike. At that time, we had a greenish outfit called fatigue clothes. Everyone looked the same, like a flock of green penguins. There was nothing to distinguish one person from another. Everybody had their hair cut mostly off, and nobody had a beard or a mustache. In this mass of men one day, I spotted my cousin, Clifford. Clifford was Uncle George's son. I didn't know that he had been drafted. Neither did he know that I was drafted. We were always close but not close enough to know what was happening in our individual lives at that time. We were young adults going about our own way in life, I guess. Here was ole Cliff. I was so surprised to see him amongst all those men! And to have met him in the company street with maybe five hundred other soldiers wandering around the same point was a surprise! It was rather incredible to me. It was the only time I ever saw Clifford while I was in the army. After the war, he returned home and ultimately died quite young. I never had another chance to see him after that one brief encounter at Fort Dix.

TRANSPORTED TO A NEW LOCATION

After spending a number of months in Fort Dix, we were all loaded aboard a train one day. We rode for hours and hours with the blinds down. We couldn't see where we were going. Everything in the military was a case of hurry up to wait or line up to stand in one spot for hours, so it was the same thing with the train. We ate and slept on that dumb train—it seemed like a month—but it probably was no more than a day or two. Finally, we pulled into a siding somewhere and a bunch of trucks came out of the dark and loaded us aboard. We rode another bunch of miles until we wound up in another tent city type of an army post. I didn't know where we were and nobody would tell us anything because that was not the way the army operated. They never told us what to expect or where we were going or where we were even coming from.

Lo and behold the next morning, bright and early, when we fell out for roll call, I looked out across the distance and saw the Washington Monument. I recognized it. I'd never seen it before, but it's hard not to recognize the Washington Monument. It was the tallest thing in the city. I knew that we were somewhere outside the city of Washington. It turned out that we were in a little army post called Rosslyn Substation in Arlington, Virginia. At that time—even though Washington is a huge place today with lots of suburbs—there were miles and miles of vacant land on the other side of the Potomac. We were on the south side of the Potomac River in the state of Virginia proper.

So there we were, back in tents. The tents were, I think, sixteen feet on the side. They were pyramid-type things with center poles. Inside the center of the tents we had the same kind of stove as in Fort Dix. It was still winter and pretty cold. These little tents did a fine job of heating those who were established *close* to the stove, but those of us who were on the perimeter walls of the tent just froze. We had no benefit from the heat at all. I even had water freeze in my canteen. That's how cold it got!

In any event, we were at least out of the snow and rain but this was nothing more than a very minimum type of an army installation. It had mud streets; everything was mud. You just couldn't walk without getting mud up to your knees. It was a case of some more training and more drilling and more whatever. But as I look back, it wasn't the worst thing ever to happen.

It wasn't anything that I'd prefer voluntarily, but it wasn't that bad really. And surprisingly enough, I met about four guys that I went to high school with while I was there. So the world sure proved itself to be small to me, even at an early age, because I kept meeting people that I knew from my younger days. It was just incredible.

As I look back on the more than half a century that's passed since my military initiation, a few things do come to mind. One was the establishment of that temporary facility. It wasn't there many more months after we departed from it. As I recall, it was removed entirely. In any event, at that time, it briefly served its purpose to quarter troops until they could be established elsewhere and distributed throughout the area.

FIREGUARD

There were other things I recall quite vividly though. One was that every night there was a fireguard. The tents were very flammable and the heat required to keep everything at a halfway decent temperature meant a lot of coal going up the chimney. That resulted in a lot of sparks. You had to be very careful that the tents didn't catch fire, particularly throughout the night when the soldiers were sleeping. I had that fire watch any number of times while I was there. I wasn't the only one on fire watch. There were several of us patrolling the camp in assigned areas.

One night in particular, two of us happened to notice that one of the tents was on fire. It went up so quickly! The guys got out; there was no problem with the men getting out of the tent. We ran over to the fire hose, which was hung up in loops outside on a rack. When we cracked the valve, we found that the pipes were frozen! We never did get that fire out and had a job keeping the fire from going to the next tent and on down the whole line of tents. Everything in that tent was destroyed including all the equipment of the soldiers.

A HARSH LESSON

We had a very minimal mess hall type of an arrangement. The mess hall didn't have windows. It was a frame building, but it had wire mesh with a plastic coating on it to keep out the weather. It didn't help much because it was very cold inside. When you ate in there, your food turned ice cold. The metal trays that you ate from and your canteen cup turned cold. And, we didn't have much to eat. I guess the Army still was not prepared for all the men that were inducted into the service at that point. A lot of guys were hungry.

One night, somebody broke into the mess hall and stole some food. The first sergeant, after learning of the theft, lined us all up that morning by a little river that ran through the post. The river was about one hundred feet wide and was covered with ice. The sergeant got down to his nubbin, right down to nothing. He just took all his clothes off and got out on the ice, jumped on it and broke through it. Then he beat his way and literally flailed his way across that river and swam back. We were all standing at attention because he didn't put us at ease through this whole display. When he got out of the river he said, "Okay, fellows, somebody stole food from the mess hall last night. Whoever it is—and if I ever catch anybody else doing it—they're going to swim this river. I wouldn't subject the men in my command to anything I wouldn't do myself." I'll never forget that because we just went hungry from then on until the conditions did ultimately improve.

SICK CALL

In my transfer from Fort Dix—where I had been given all my required inoculations—to Rosslyn Substation, my medical records became lost in the shuffle. I didn't lose them. The military did. Therefore I had to have the whole series of shots all over. This resulted in my having severe constipation. Reporting to sick call was not easy as so many GIs used it as an excuse to avoid duty. Thus, the sergeants took a dim view of placing you on the sick call list if you looked okay. My constipation became critical and in efforts to ease the condition, I wound up with a hemorrhoid of enormous size that really put me out of action. If there had been a P.X. or access to a pharmacy I would have handled my own problem, but all the while we were posted in that camp we were restricted from leaving for any reason. In fact, it was many weeks before we were allowed off the post to go to Washington. My second effort to go on sick call was finally granted. The doctor treated the hemorrhoid, but I sure suffered for many weeks.

NEW BARRACKS

I don't recall how long I stayed in Rosslyn Substation. It wasn't for a prolonged period of time because one day they loaded us all into trucks again and took us to South Post, Fort Myer, which is also in Virginia on the outskirts of Washington. In fact it was an old Civil War post. The north part of the post was still a Cavalry post then. Even though horses were no longer used in combat, the Army did keep a Cavalry detachment there to perform all of the military burials for the higher-ranking people who were buried with more military honors than the typical GI was accorded.

We were quartered in a brand new barracks. I mean brand, spanking new. The barracks wasn't anything more than just a wood framed shell with a roof and windows. It still didn't have a heating system at the time we took it over. The barracks had these magnificent pine floors! They weren't painted or varnished or treated; they were just raw wood floors. And here we came across the compound, which was thick with mud. There was no grass on the ground or gravel on the streets. After we had traipsed through the mud we went clunking through this barracks, and everybody was just leaving tracks like you can't believe on this beautiful pine floor. I was hoping I wouldn't be the one assigned to clean it.

In our new barracks we were assigned bunks and footlockers. After we organized our bedding, hung up our clothes, or put them away in the footlockers, we were told to fall out. We had changed our clothes and boots because all of us were covered in mud and were wet and cold. We went back outside for whatever reason and, after a little bit we were dismissed and brought back into the barracks. When we got back inside, we were told we had to scrub the floors. So that's what we did. Everybody got these GI brushes, soap, and water. We went down on our knees and scrubbed and mopped and got that floor spotless. There were several hundred men that had come in and out of that barracks. After we got the floor all nice and clean and our equipment cleaned up, we were told to fall out. It was time for a drill or whatever exercises we were to go through. Afterward, we came back into the barracks and got the floor all muddy again. Of course we were ordered to scrub the floors a second time. We did this day in and day out. Every time we left and came back in, we had to clean the barracks and scrub the floors. That got pretty dad-burned old, but that's the way the military functioned. They had a bunch of soldiers who were yet unassigned to any specific duties, and they had to keep us occupied. And the food was much better in our new location. We were now eating in mess halls that were heated, and the food was pretty good. I couldn't complain. Army food agreed with me well enough. And many guys who had not had enough to eat during the Depression could now count on three square meals a day.

PRIVATE NABBE AT FORT MYER, VIRGINIA
1944

BECOMING A CHAUFFEUR

I wasn't in Fort Myer very long when I was assigned to the Motor Pool, which was then operating out of the Pentagon. The Motor Pool facility, a raw concrete cavern, was about two levels below grade. The Pentagon was not finished. It was still windowless. It was just a huge shell and hull of a building. Anticipating the function of the Pentagon as a center of the military activities, the Motor Pool was an integral part of that because we chauffeured officers back and forth between the War Department in Washington and the Pentagon in Virginia.

I was trained then as a chauffeur and a truck driver. I had to take all kinds of training so I could drive all different kinds of vehicles. I had a military license that qualified me to drive quite a few different types of equipment. One of the first things I drove was a large bus about the size of a school bus. I drove this bus on a regular route from the Pentagon to the War Department in Washington where I would load up with officers that I took to the Pentagon. I then turned around and took a bunch of others back to the War Department. This went on all day, day in and day out for quite a while.

Then I was taken off that duty and given an extended stretch vehicle. It was a standard Chevrolet or Plymouth sedan with a hunk added in the middle so that you had seating for six to ten people. That was a little strange to drive. You had to swing quite wide to get around some of the corners because of the long wheelbase. It was even more difficult for me to drive that big car than it was to drive the bus. I also drove this on a fixed route, ferrying officers back and forth.

Little by little I was introduced into the huge military complexes. Through the Pentagon Garage we handled all of the officers from all the branches of the military—the Navy Department, the Air Force, etc. As my experience broadened and I was given more and more assignments, I drove further and further away from my home base. Eventually I reached the point where I drove out of the Washington area and stayed overnight at different army posts.

I don't recall how long I was at the Pentagon when I was transferred into the city of Washington to what, at that time, was called the C Street Barracks. They were not too far from the Lincoln Memorial. We were attached to the

War Department Motor Pool Garage several blocks from the barracks. It was a building that took up a whole block. It was a round one-story building of brick built prior to the Civil War where the horses and carriages were maintained for the White House. In due time it was converted into a garage, long before we were assigned there. We operated from that point as it gave us a more central location.

DRIVING THE BRASS

Next I was assigned to drive officers. It certainly wasn't meant to be any kind of an honor. It's just that I was trusted to do a more intricate level of work, finding my way to a multitude of military installations, some of which were almost secret, kept out of the public eye so to speak. It was most interesting. I got to know quite a few people and got to see a lot of the country that I guess the poor guy who was assigned to one single job never did get to experience.

PERKS OF THE JOB

The C Street Barracks were very convenient to the city of Washington and, of course, the city treated all service personnel with a great deal of deference. They were very, very kind to those of us serving in any branch of the service. The U.S.O. and the theaters gave servicemen free movie tickets, and boxing matches were free as well. We had free food, free drink, and free cigarettes. There was a lot of recreational potential for anybody who had the off-duty time to enjoy it. When I was stationed so close to all that entertainment, it was a real bonanza for me because I didn't have any money to speak of. Our pay at that time was about twenty-one dollars a month. Out of that came insurance, laundry, and a few other things. I didn't have a lot of money for off-duty pleasures.

INCIDENT IN THE BARRACKS

Living in the city barracks was almost like living in a dormitory. I was assigned to an upper bunk, and I fell out of the dumb thing. I rolled out of bed in the middle of the night because I was a restless sleeper. I wasn't injured, but I asked the sergeant in charge if I could have a lower bunk. They were, of course, the preferred bunks. The older guys—the guys with the seniority—were assigned to those.

The sergeant didn't reassign me and subsequently, I fell out of that dumb bunk again. This time I came down hard and busted the living heck out of my lips and ripped my flesh loose from my lower jaw. I had quite a bit of stitch work. They took me to Walter Reed Hospital in the middle of the night, and the doctor told me that because of the nerve endings in my lips, it would be very difficult to insert any kind of Novocaine or local anesthetic. He said he was going to have to sew me up without it. I didn't have much of an option about the treatment. When he began sewing, I don't think anything but my heels and the back of my head were on that operating table because the rest of me was an arch! You could have rolled a watermelon underneath my back at any point. That hurt; boy did that hurt! Of course my front teeth got bent in and they thought for a minute that they were going to have to remove them, but they pulled them straight and they did stiffen back up in time. After I came back, I was reassigned to a lower bunk. That was the one advantage of the mishap.

TRANSFER TO THE PENTAGON

I don't have a recollection of when I was transferred back to the Pentagon Motor Pool Garage, but by this time the building was finished and pretty well occupied. Finishing the construction of the Pentagon was accelerated by the need of the war effort. They worked on it day and night until it was totally completed. At this time I was still living in the C Street Barracks, but I was working out of the Pentagon. Every morning the truck would come, and we'd all load in it and drive over to the Pentagon. We did that for quite a while.

C STREET MOTOR POOL, ORIGINALLY STABLES
FOR THE WHITE HOUSE DURING THE CIVIL
WAR ERA.

RICHARD GETS DRAFTED

Prior to my brother, Richard, being drafted I had to drive a major or light colonel up to the ordnance school in Aberdeen, Maryland. Richard still hadn't been inducted into the Army. I mentioned to this officer that it would be a shame for him to become an infantryman and get himself blown apart because he was a good tool and die maker. The officer took my name and address. Subsequently, I got a letter from him, which I was to give to Richard. It said that Richard should report directly to Aberdeen, Maryland when he was inducted. Of course, I felt pretty good about that. I thought that I was hopefully sparing my bother harm by his being in less of a combat position. But as the war progressed, it turned out that Richard did get into more combat than he cared ever to talk about.

THE PURLOINED PASS

Eventually, Richard, too, was drafted by the Army. When he was stationed in Aberdeen, he took off one weekend to come visit with me in the C Street Barracks. We went out and had a couple of beers together. We were sitting in the tavern enjoying ourselves when the MPs came in. Richard said, "Boy, I'm in trouble." I asked, "What's wrong?" He said, "I don't have a pass. I'm A.W.O.L." (Absent without leave). Well, it just so happened that I had earlier come across some blank passes. I had conscripted them for emergencies when I saw they were available. I said, "Fear not, Brother." I wrote him a pass using some fictitious officer's name and gave it to him. When the M.P.s came along and checked me I was okay because I had a permanent fifty-mile pass. Then they glanced at Richard's. They didn't detect that anything was awry so they went on to the next guy. Richard didn't wind up in any trouble in the tavern and went back to his camp. But, when he got back there he got caught and was in trouble for having been A.W.O.L.

AN UNUSUAL TRAIN RIDE

Later that night I rode back as far as Baltimore, Maryland on a train with Richard. That was as far as my fifty-mile pass would allow me to go. Richard had to continue on to Aberdeen on that same train. Somewhere between Washington and Baltimore, we were standing in the coach. Being wartime, all kinds of old equipment were on the lines. Everything was jammed to the rafters with people and service personnel going back and forth. And, because the coaches were jam-packed, we were standing in a vestibule. All of a sudden these big rocks started flying up through gaps in the plates in the floor and rattling around inside. That, to me, was most unusual. I looked down and I could see a big piece of equipment dragging off the bottom of the train. It was ripping the ties and slamming these rocks up at us. I told Richie, "You go one way and see if you can find a conductor and I'll go the other way. Tell him that we've got problems with this train." I met a conductor before Richie did, and I told him, "There's something dragging underneath the train." The guy didn't even bother to go check it. He just stopped the train. He pulled a cord and that train came to a grinding halt. Sure enough, a big piece of the underbody of the train somehow had broken loose and was dragging. They had to take the car off and put it on a siding. All the people on that car had to jam into the remaining coaches, making Richard's and my ride to Aberdeen quite uncomfortable with too many people all jammed together.

We were quite late getting to Baltimore and I had just barely enough time to turn around, catch a train, and go back to my own post before I was A.W.O.L. Richard went on the rest of the way and got nailed for being away without a pass. That was the way it was. I guess you took your chances when you were still clinging to what you knew as a kid. Richard and I were always very close, and while the war ended up separating us by an ocean, we kept in constant contact.

RICHARD

While my brother, Richard, was overseas, we corresponded religiously. I saved all of his letters. Of course, much of Richard's letters went through censorship so he couldn't be too specific about military goings on. He was quite graphic in many of his letters as he related what was happening in Europe. Here I was on the safe side of the war while he was on the dangerous side. Somewhere in between the two is a balance. I don't know where it exists, but as old history concludes and all the forces and factors are analyzed, there seems to be a balance in it.

Richard never gave me a chronological accounting. Rather he would talk briefly on rare occasions about the combat end of his exposure in the European Theater of Operations. As with most veterans who knew first hand the horrors of war, it seemed to be too painful for him to describe, especially in detail. At times when he was drunk or amused he would voluntarily tell me a few things. Any probing I would do would be met by silence. Much of the less gruesome episodes were told in his letters to me. Of the things he did orally relate in brief detail was hitting the beach at Omaha where he and his buddy were rushing ashore under fire. He told me he turned to his buddy to say something in time to see a shell take off his head. The body stumbled forward a few more steps and then fell frontward.

Richard also told me he had been assigned to a Ranger group. The outfit he was originally trained within the beginning was an ordnance company who perished when their vessel was sunk in the invasion. He told me an officer approached the Ranger group prior to their on-shore assault asking if there were any ex-ordnance men in the outfit. Richard acknowledged that he was and went off with the officer while the Rangers assaulted the bluffs. Richard said the Rangers were wiped out so he escaped in two ways—by not being with the ordnance outfit that perished and lastly by being recalled from the Rangers who went forward to their own glory.

Richard related another time when his army group surrounded a Nazi army who refused to surrender. In response the U.S. Army leveled every gun at the Nazis and blew the Nazis to pieces. When Richard's outfit went into the battle zone most every German body was in bits and pieces. Richard told me he picked up a German helmet to send to me only to find the cap of the dead soldier's skull inside. He mentioned the foregoing in a very pained way and shuddered in the retelling of the hideous episode.

Another time Richard had R & R (rest and recuperation) and for the first time in weeks had a chance to sleep in a feather bed in the upstairs of a Belgian farmhouse. During the night the house was hit by a shell and Richard got blown outside but was unharmed. He complained that the first chance he had gotten to have a clean comfortable bed and a good night's sleep was short-lived.

Pfc. Richard Nabbe 32920618
COE 14th Bat., 4th Reg't.
Camp Reynolds
Greenville, PA
Building T-2033

Pfc. Robert Nabbe
Motor Center Detach.
2131 "C" St. N.W.
Washington, D.C.

December 28, 1943
Dear Rob;

Just a line to let you know that by some stroke of good fortune I am not in the guard house. I got in three hours and ½ A.W.O.L. but everything turned out all right and I didn't even get company duty. They sure rush your fanny off around here. When I got back I went on 24 hour guard duty. Rob believe me it's no fun walking four posts. You think you will never get done. Today we drilled all morning, did exercises (with overcoats on), played football, went to the movies, got a lecture on first aid, ran an obstacle course, did a supply detail and etc. To-morrow I'm on special detail. Quite a busy day, eh? Wal, so it goes I guess. I'll have to put up with it for the time being. This place is little Pittsburg. We use soft coal and everything is black with soot. It's also cold as hell. Enough of this bitching at present.

I want you to know how happy I was to be home with you folks Christmas. I never expected it but it was worth all I did to get home. I'd like you to know how I appreciate your gift and I'm sorry I couldn't return one. You know how it goes Rob. That sure was a swell dinner we had. I can sure appreciate it from the chow we get here. Also it has taken me two days to get over a slight hangover I got while home. I feel pretty good now though.

I spend all my spare time going to movies; it keeps me from going nuts. I'll be all up on them all by the time I leave here. Quite an accomplishment. I guess you had enough of misery because you probably have plenty of your own. So — so long for a bit and thanks again.

Your Brother
Rich

P.S. I got another shot too! Oooooooh

Pfc. Richard Nabbe 32920618
COE 14th Bat., 4th Reg't.
Camp Reynolds
Greenville, PA
Building T-2033

Pfc. Robert Nabbe
Motor Center Detach.
2131 "C" St. N.W.
Washington, D.C.

Thursday, Dec 29, 1943
Dear Rob;

I had a feeling you wouldn't fail me and write a letter to me. It's the first letter I got since I left on furlough. I had a path beaten to the Day Room looking for mail. So you see I highly appreciate it.

As I previously wrote I was 3 ½ hours AWOL[1] but all came out all right. Just a piece of Nabbe luck I guess. As you know, Pop did hurt my feelings quite a bit. However, I feel he didn't realize it so all is forgiven. I never felt as bad in all my life as I did when he started sounding off. It was so unnecessary and especially on poor Dot[2] who never causes any harm. I have a great regard for her Rob and I can't stand having anyone picking on her especially when she does no wrong. She treats us swell and works like a dog to please us when we are home so you see that anyone with an ounce of feeling wouldn't like to see her abused. Especially you know how easy it is to hurt her. Oh well, I guess the strain of traveling so long and anticipation just got the best of me. I'm sorry if I caused a bad impression but sometimes you can't help it. It still proves I'm human regardless of what some people think.

I know how the trains are Rob because I had the same trouble here. You have to expect that on the holidays I guess.

I guess I won't be home again for a long time but you folks are always on my heart and I'll never forget you regardless of what happens. I got a second shake down today and we had to try on all brand new equipment. Everything has to fit perfectly too or it's no go. Looks like it won't be long now.

We just got 300 new men in and it's sure a relief. Maybe now they can ease up on

---

1 AWOL means Absent Without Leave, a military term for a soldier who has left his station without permission.
2 Dot is Dorothy Lois Nabbe, Robert and Richard's younger sister.

the details. I hope so because I'll be worn out if they don't

Well Rob, I must fall out now so I'll say so long. I don't need any money but thanx anyhow. Please write again cause it's so good to hear from you.

Bye for now.

Your Brother

Rich

P.S. I'm equally proud!!

I did see Richard one more time before he was transported overseas to the European Theater. He got a furlough to get home and I was fortunate enough to get a pass. I guess it was a two-day pass, the best that I could manage. It used to take me darn near six or seven hours to get home and the same amount of time to get back, so I didn't have a lot of time at home to visit. It was just that I had to see Richard as often as I could because who knew what his fate would be once he got over to Europe in the battle zone. And I suppose as his older brother, I always felt like his protector as I had done so many times when we were kids.

In any event, we were all together at my parents' home in Irvington, New Jersey. Our father was jawboning our sister Dorothy about something, and he got Dorothy crying. My mother began crying. Then Richard started crying. Richard became visibly upset. He said to our father, "You know, this is an awful thing to have happen. This will be my last memory of home. Who knows if I'll ever get back? It's an awful thing." But it didn't seem to bother my father. He was indifferent about anybody's feelings except his own.

About the same period of time, John Tobin, my fiancée Margie's brother, happened to be in Washington. John was in the Coast Guard. He looked me up, and we spent a day together. I have a picture of John standing in front of the Lincoln Memorial. He stayed with me in the C Street Barracks located quite close to Lincoln Memorial. We didn't have very far to go to find a good backdrop for a family photograph. That was the only time that I saw John until after the war was over, and we all got back together again in New Jersey.

PRIVATE NABBE, FIRST TRIP HOME,
WINTER 1943

PRIVATE FIRST CLASS

I was working back and forth between the old White House stable garage and the Pentagon. I don't recall exactly at what point I was one place or another. I do know that I divided quite a bit of time between the two. I progressed to a point where I was promoted to Private First Class. There weren't many ratings in our outfit, and there were several hundred men. There was one master sergeant, a tech sergeant, a couple of buck sergeants, and a mechanic who was a sergeant. Everybody else was usually a private or a Private First Class. My assignment wasn't the type of military function that allowed a lot of promotions, so I was pleased to be recognized for my service. Best of all, I got a raise of four dollars a month. It wasn't a lot of money, but back in those days, a dollar did go a lot further. It was 1943, and I was driving only officers now. I wasn't driving jeeps or trucks anymore. My Private First Class rating made me strictly a chauffeur for officers. There were enough other people to drive the motorcycles and Jeeps. They transported civilians and War Department employees, but I was assigned to only drive officers.

As I look back I realize that driving strictly officers was a leg up on what the rest of the outfit was doing. I had clean clothes and was even issued additional uniforms. I had five sets of suntans for the summer and several blouses and two or three pairs of wool trousers for my winter uniform. Looking neat in appearance was a requisite for the type of work that I was doing, and I had a lot of clothes issued me for just that reason. It was a promotion, and I was glad to get it.

RETRIBUTION—GI STYLE

Every outfit seemed to have one bully who delighted in intimidating anyone he could. The one in our platoon was a semi-bald chap close to thirty years in age, much older than the majority of the troops. He was six feet tall weighing about 180 pounds and was quite a bit larger than most of the men. He was also a physical fitness nut who used spring tension exercise equipment he kept stored in his footlocker. Each day after supper he would go through his exercise routine. The guy always seemed to have a perpetual chip on his shoulder. He already had been in several fights usually with smaller opponents. This time as expected, he got into it with a smaller fellow who was hardly his match, but who also had enough pride to stand up to the bully. It wasn't a fair contest and the smaller chap took a pounding.

It wasn't long after the incident when the bully and I were transferred to night duty with our sleep time during the day when the barracks were empty. There were five of us on this shift and as coincidence would have it, my bunk and the bully's were one bunk apart. Sleeping was arranged so that men slept head to toe. Every other bunk bed had the sleeper's head to the wall. The intervening bunks had the sleeper's head at the aisle end. This way men weren't breathing into each other's faces and possibly passing along cold and flu bugs.

Some men have long memories, as was the case with the bully's smaller opponent who was still on the day shift. This chap managed to return to the near empty barracks just after we had retired. The bully had fallen asleep quickly. I knew because I heard him snoring. I was just about to drift off myself when I sensed someone was near my bunk. Normally we had a full-time barracks orderly present for policing the place and monitoring the facility against intruders because the C Street Barracks were directly in the city. I thought the person standing near my bunk was the barracks orderly which would have been quite normal. Opening my eyes slightly I saw it was the bully's recent opponent. I continued to feign sleep, and once the soldier confirmed that I wasn't the man he was seeking, he moved on to the bully's bunk. Sure of his target, he took a heavy GI boot and smashed it squarely across the bully's face. Then, he beat a hasty retreat. Fortunately for him the barracks orderly was on the second floor so the event had only me as a witness. I quickly sat up, and making eye contact with the perpetrator as he scurried down the aisle, I placed my finger to my lips and eyes to indicate I hadn't seen or heard a thing.

Our resident bully was a bloody mess with split lips and eventual black eyes and swollen face that marked him for quite a few days. When the barracks orderly did come in a short while after the bashing, he called the orderly room at the garage and in a minute the place was a mass of confusion. I was "awakened" and told to dress and to report immediately to the Commanding Officer where I was thoroughly questioned. I said I did not see or hear a thing as I had worked hard the night before and had fallen asleep promptly. I'm sure they suspected I was covering up for the assailant, but they couldn't prove anything. Later on when I saw the avenger, I assured him that his secret was safe with me and that I thought the bully got what he rightfully deserved all factors considered.

TIME OFF

One of the advantages of living in the C Street Barracks, which was not too far from the center of Washington, the White House, and the commercial district, was that the work I did had fairly regular hours. I would put in an eight or ten hour shift. If I was on day duty I was free in the evening. A lot of times I had Sunday off. I used that time to visit the Smithsonian Institution and all the nice art galleries and museums that were in Washington. It was very interesting. Fortunately the streetcar system was widespread. You could go every place for a small amount of money, a dime or twenty cents. The streetcar would get you all over the area that I was stationed in. It was called the Military District of Washington. The outfit that I was with was the Motor Center Detachment of the 2525th Service Unit.

PRIVATE NABBE (LEFT) WITH TWO BUDDIES,
FT. MYER, VIRGINIA, 1944

Pfc. Richard Nabbe 32920618
COE 14th Bat., 4th Reg't.
Camp Reynolds
Greenville, PA
Building T-2033

Pfc. Robert Nabbe
Motor Center Detachment
2131 C St. N.W.
Washington, D.C.

January 6, 1944

Dear Rob,

Well I am still here. I don't even know how long. I may be here for a few days and maybe a month yet. We can't tell a darned thing around this joint.

Your new job sounds like the one I just left. Quite a nice little racket you have. I hope you hang on to it for a while. If you ever leave that job and get into a place like this, you will rue the day you left. Just like I'm doing.

I'm getting used to this place now. We hike about 11 or 12 miles a day and believe me with all the drilling it's a real strain on you. My muscles are still a bit stiff but gradually they are feeling better.

Speaking of snow we haven't a bit here now. It has been raining here quite frequently and all of it has washed away. Today it has grown much colder and windy but is nice and clear. We so seldom see the sun that it's quite a treat when it does come out.

Speaking of Leo[3], don't worry about Dot Rob; she knows what she is doing. I think nothing will come of it. He's due for shipment soon and that will be that. I hope - As far as having him for a brother in law, I don't approve of it myself much.

Say, if you like ice skating, this is the place to do it. We have a great big river and plenty of other places in reserve. And as far as being cold enough, well, you can use your own judgment.

I sure remember those old days and I'm not one to forget them either. Well comes the end of the war and we'll do all those things again. Till then we'll just have to reminisce and be contented.

---

3   Leo is Leon Smith, the man Dorothy later married (October 1948)

That was a nice long letter you wrote me and I had a great deal of pleasure reading it. That's about all we have to look forward to here, is mail.

Well Rob, thanks again and keep 'em coming. When I do ship, I'll let you know. Till then take it easy. You probably will any-how. Bye

Your Brother

Rich

Pfc. Richard Nabbe 32920618
COE 14th Bat., 4th Reg't.
Camp Reynolds
Greenville, Pa
Building T-2033

Pfc. Robert Nabbe
Motor Center Detachment
2131 C St. N.W.
Washington, D.C.

January 13, 1943 [sic][4]

Dear Rob;

I received your letter today and in appreciation I am answering right back.

I just got off a ten mile hike and am whiffed out. Instead of better, it gets worse around here. After working all day, I go on fire guard at 12:00 tonight and work till 8:00 tomorrow morning. All we get is details. Honest to god if I stay here much longer I'm going over the hill. I have to talk myself out of it now. All you do is work around this cursed hole. They never let up on a guy. I can see now why even the chaplains go over the hill too. That's not just talk either believe me. I hope to leave here this week, but you just can't tell. I may be stuck here for a month yet. I pray to god it isn't so.

I heard about Johnny O[5]*, and believe me it sure was a shock. Just think how it will be if anymore of the boys get knocked off. It's a god damned shame in plain English. Gee, I bet his mother feels terrible. I know how Mom would feel if one of us got it. I wrote his mother a letter of sympathy and as you said, it was crude but it may help a bit. It's so hard to try to say anything in a case like that.*

We went on a ten mile hike today and then they go and stick me on KP this afternoon. I got off at three o'clock and am hiding in the barracks till retreat. 4:30 your time (mine too). Oh well, who gives a good xxcccxxxcc. I can't understand why my mail

---

4   Richard dates the letter January 13, 1943, but the actual date was 1944. The postmark on the front of the letter denotes the letter was mailed January 13, 1944.

5   Johnny O. is John O'Connor, next-door neighbor in Irvington. He was Robert and Richard's first friend to die in World War II. Robert says, "I wrote his family also and have kept a response from his mother."

isn't coming through. Yours seems to get here all right and I answer right back all the time. Guess the mail service is lousy around here.

So you are in the Army 13 months, eh? I bet it seems like 13 years to you. It seems like 9 years to me. Well Rob don't worry, the war will be over in 1950 or so. Ain't I an optimist? I should be better dead you mean. Hey, take it easy on that fighting bud. You may catch a court marshal for that. Now you wouldn't want a discharge would you? (Oh Brother).

I wish the hell they would make up their mind as to what they are going to do with you guys. I know it gets monotonous as hell doing the same thing day out and day in, so maybe if you do get shipped you'd like it better. Let's hope you stay. You got Margie[6] to come back to and I haven't, so you better try to hang onto what you have.

I don't go out much because connections for transportation are so bad. Also it's to damned cold to be waiting or a bus. First we have to walk a mile to the bus station and get a bus to Sharon, then we have to get a bus to Youngstown. Two hours round trip. That makes four hours coming and going providing you get good connections. So you see it takes most of your time getting there and then worrying if you get back or not. I did get to Cleveland, Ohio with a fellow. I pal with him here and had a good time. We got in camp at 5'oclock Monday morning and got an hours sleep before reveille. It was worth it though. This guy lends me his car to take a broad out with and I got lost in Cleveland and couldn't find his house again. I burned up 5 gallons of his gas before I finally did find it. Then it was a mistake. He didn't like the idea that I burned up all his gas but he was lucky I got back at all. We left Cleveland (85) miles from here, and got back in 1 hr 30 min. Our wheels never touched the ground all the way in. He should take out a pilot's license.

(12:00 the same night) Well here I am on fire guard. I have five fires to look after till tomorrow morning. We have a wonderful baker here and he is stuffing me with some cakes he just made. A real swell guy too. The cake is delicious. No wonder, it's officer mess. Of course you realize the quality of food differs to quite an extent between the two. Ours and this. And so into the wee hours of the morning I go.

Hey Rob! You know that snow you were supposed to get? Well we're getting it here I'm afraid. It's been snowing for the last three days. On and off of course. A flurry here and there. What worries me is that it may start and forget to stop. It will be very funny to go on a ten mile hike. Ha! Ha! Am I laughing? NO. The baker just left me with a big pile of pots and pans to wash. My buddie!

---

6   Marjorie May Tobin Nabbe, Robert's wife. Marjorie and Robert married on October 10, 1943. Robert wore his army uniform and Marjorie wore a white satin dress that she and her sister, Jessie, crafted.

Say, how do you like my uphill writing? Unique isn't it? I don't know how I do it but it happens every time.

I haven't had a word from Alby L.[7] in a long time. I did drop him a card but I don't know if it will bring any results or not. I'd like to hear from him. I alone can appreciate your feeling pertaining to a gab fest to Mrs. Laver. I know what torture is. My advice is to shun all contact. Comprendé?

Well Rob that's all the grief I can put on paper in one time so I guess I'll end it all. I don't mean commit suicide but end this literary monstrosity.

Thanks for the (ahem) contribution old boy. I can use it, I assure you. However Rob, I can get along ok. I don't want you to send me any money as I know you can use it yourself. You don't get any more than I do. "A requested favor". If you can get any V127 film, please pick it up for me immediately if not sooner. Please inform me as to if so and where and etc. All efforts greatly appreciated. Bye now kid, and write again.

Your Brother
Rich

---

7   Alby L. is Albert Laver, an early friend who lived nearby (the Nabbe's and Alby's rear yards abutted). Robert states, "Mrs. Laver was a gabber. If she caught my mom in the rear yard, it was yak-yak-yak."

A WAR-TIME WEDDING

Before I was drafted, I worked at Weston Electric Company. It was there that I met the prettiest girl in the bunch, Marjorie Tobin. It was early 1941, and I finally got the courage to ask her for a date. We clicked and by the time I was drafted, we were pretty well committed to each other. And like many thousands of other young couples across America, we ended up in a long distance relationship. We became engaged, and I gave her a diamond ring that my father had set for me. A highly skilled tool and die maker, Dad did jewelry work on the side from home. I felt great about my circumstances. I had a wonderful fiancée, and a highly prized job in the army as a chauffeur to high-ranking officers.

One of the advantages of having a fairly stable job in the Army was that I had the best of everything. The proximity to home allowed me to visit my fiancée frequently—not every weekend, but as often as I could get away. I used to sneak home because I only had a fifty-mile pass and, of course, getting back to New Jersey was two hundred miles. I took a lot of chances, but I never got caught. I was pretty lucky about that.

I hated being away from Margie, and while she wrote me letters regularly, it wasn't as satisfying as spending time together. Even though we knew our separation would continue until I was discharged, we decided that we would get married on my first furlough. I, of course, couldn't anticipate when that was going to happen. We patiently waited, and I finally did get a week's furlough in October, 1943. Margie and I got married on the tenth, and took a short honeymoon in the Pocono Mountains of Pennsylvania. After that, I returned less than enthusiastic to the military arrangement that I was established in as opposed to the bliss that I knew with my new wife.

PFC. Richard Nabbe
Co K, 9th Group
Camp Reynolds
Greenville, Pa.

January 21, 1944

Dear Rob

*Well old soak I received your letter and I'll have you know I laughed like hell at
it. Boy you have an awful lot of trouble don't you? How you get into all those jams is
beyond me. Anyhow Rob, it's an experience and although it isn't funny at the time, it
sure brings back sweet memories.*

*Hey that four days to get a letter from me is a crock of shit. Somebody must be
reading it en route or something. Also, they are taking their good natured time about
shipping me out of here too. The bastards!! They love to see me suffer I guess.*

*I got a racket now though. I hope it lasts till I get out of here. We have four fire-
men on now, so I only work 8 hrs and I'm off 24. Ah, is that sweet. I'll bet somebody
will get wind of it and screw the whole business. Eight hours at that job is a snap.
So you were a fireman too eh? Wal you should look at your n***** of a brother and
pray I never get so dirty in my life as I get here. We specialize in soft coal here so don't
complain. Boy what a dirty place this is. Well I'll get even. I'll eat that damned old mess
hall dry when I go on shift. I can't eat their rotten old food in the daytime so I'll get even
at night. I'm a coal man commando, an ice box raider. No extra pay involved.*

*I might as well tell you and get it over with, I bought the camera off that guy for
$30. I know what you are thinking and you are probably right. But you know me and
you also know why I want the film. I'd like to take some pictures of this hole for future
reference if you know what I mean. I want to spit on them at random. Keep trying will
you sweetheart. I tried all over and it's no dice. You can't buy a darned thing out here.*

*We haven't had any snow here for the last couple of weeks. (am I sorry) I hear the
whole coast had snow. My deepest sympathies old boy. Poor Joe⁸, I bet he has a lot of fun
too. How the hell is Sid Freund⁹? I haven' seen him in a dogs age. I bet he's having a lot
of fun. So Sliker¹⁰ is a captain eh? Boy he sure gets places don't he. It must be great to*

---

8   Joe is Joe Urban. Robert states, "As a very new boy on the block, my new neighbor,
     Leonard Neurenberg, introduced me to Joe who greeted me with 'Hello you son-of-a-
     bitch.' A very amusing introduction but we became lifelong friends."
9   Sid Freund was a friend from Richard and Robert's youth.
10   Sliker is Larry Sliker, another childhood friend.

have a brain.

So your meals are lousy too eh? Well Rob, do like I do and spend what meager pay you have on decent food. I'm broke now so I'll have to eat the shit they call food I guess! I go to Youngstown and get a decent meal whenever I can. A great morale booster.

I don't blame you for saving your money Rob. If I was married, I'd do the same thing. It must be swell to have a home of your own. I admire you and Margie's thoughtfulness in thinking of me and I appreciate it a lot. However, when you start getting a raft of kids I think you will change your mind. I could use a retreat though. It sure would come in handy!!!!

I got a nice reply from Mrs. O'Conner and I think she was nice in doing so. Poor woman, I know how she must feel. I got a letter from Alby too and he's thinking of joining the navy. He had better think it over if you ask me! If he gets a commission though, it won't be bad!

I had a date with a broad in Youngstown last nite and she stood me up. Wal, be unto her if I meet her again. I'll put concrete up her ass for revenge. Oh how I mistrust the un-fair sex. Phooey on em! Well, I took my last few aft-pence and got drunk so I got that much out of it anyway.

Wal Rob, I haven't a damned thing to say so I'll bid thee fare well. Keep on writing because I really enjoy your letters. They cheer me up… See what you can do about the film and stay sober. If you stay as sober as me, forget about it! By for now

Your brother

Rob

P.S. You should see the way they are slaughtering the dogs around here. It's awful! The bastards should try shooting Japs instead of poor defenseless mutts.

P. S. We had quite an article in the Cleveland paper about your W.A D. Lieutenant. Woo! Woo!

PFC. Richard Nabbe
Co K, 9th Group
Camp Reynolds
Greenville, Pa.[11]

Pfc. Robert Nabbe
Motor Center Detach.
2131 "C" St. N.W.
Washington, D.C.

January 26, 1944

Dear Rob;

Beyond a doubt, your letters are the most interesting and comical ones I ever received. You can't imagine how much I enjoy reading them. I don't know where in the hell you get all the experiences from but you certainly do have them. On the contrary, I don't seem to have much luck at all, as far as interesting items go, around here. Of course, you have to take into consideration your situation. In Washington most anything can happen.

So you are still chopping off the lard, eh? Well I wish I could do the same, but it hangs right with me. Maybe that's because I'm still a kitchen commando as a night fireman.

You know I must have a magnetic hand because all my writing seems to go uphill. I'll have to figure that on out some day.

Your kid brother has been a sick "Wittle Wabbit" for the past week. And I mean sick. I've got an awful cold. My throat has been so sore I can't even swallow. I've taken to sucking lemons and gargling with salt water and it does seem to have made a marked improvement.

Also I have been struck by another bit of misfortune too. The other night the fickle finger of fate started playing around with my wristwatch and I lost it. Now I have to tell time by the stars. Seeing how it's cloudy as hell most of the time here abouts, I'm stuck as far as time goes. All attempts for recovery have been in vain. With these guys around here, you could lose your head and they wouldn't return it. Most of my time is spent

---

11　　This letter was written on letterhead with the obverse of the Coat of Arms of the United States (it appears on the one dollar bill). Underneath the eagle this address appears: Shenango Personnel Replacement Depot, Transfer, Pennsylvania followed by P. O. Address: Greenville, Pennsylvania.

trying to recover from this cold. Of course there are other varied reasons. One mainly is I am broke as I ever hope to be. Nothing unusual. And two is they are getting chicken shit about passes.

I got two rolls of film from Dot so loaded the camera and every time the sun shines I run like hell outside and snap a picture. I'll have a roll used up pretty soon and I send it home. From its contents (If they turn out) you can derive a picture of this lovely place. I'm anxious to see the results, if any. The camera is small and compact and takes 16 exposures. It's the nut for what I want and I'm not sorry I bought it. By the way it's a "Forth Darby" or something like that. Thanks for all the trouble you went through Rob. If you can't get any, give up. I think I have a lead on some in Cleveland. (This conversation is about film.)

Christ don't tell me you'll be out of Washington in 30 days. Wow what is this army coming to. Everybody moves around but we never get anywhere. What a situation.

Well chum as I related to you previously, I haven't much to say because of circumstances beyond my control. However its a few lines anyway so you'll have to be contented. BE good and say hello to all the WAACys for me. (as if you haven't you Charleton)

If I ship I'll let you know quick like.

Your Brother
Rich

I'll be awaiting your mail in the future, old tops.

SUPPLEMENTING MY INCOME

One of the big department stores had part-time work available— particularly close to Christmas—for people who wanted to come in and wrap gift packages. Our outfit allowed that those of us who wanted to could work there. I took a job there to make a few extra bucks. It was nice, clean work. I wrapped packages from about seven o'clock at night to eleven. It was just a short ride back to the barracks, so I got my normal range of sleep. When you consider that in the army they blew the whistle in your ear around five-thirty or six o'clock, it was important to get enough rest to keep from falling asleep while driving a vehicle.

A HORRIFIC EVENT

As I look back, I recall a few incidences that were out of the ordinary. The rest of my daily routine was just chauffeuring. I drove to many different cities and in many different directions. I remember one gruesome incident in particular. It got burned in my memory because I was an eyewitness to a large military aircraft crashing. I had driven a brigadier general who was taking his staff from Bolling Air Field. It was out there next to his aircraft parked on the apron that the incident happened. I was unloading camera equipment that was going along with the general. Bolling Field and Anacosta Naval Air Station were end-to-end and were separated by a low five-foot chain link fence on the boundary of the two fields.

I heard this large aircraft taking off, so I looked over and saw that it was a naval plane. I learned later that it was loaded with high-ranking Naval and Marine Corp officers. As the aircraft was rising off the ground, it barely cleared the fence. The motors were making an awful racket and I knew right away that that plane was in trouble. Very gradually, the plane rolled over, and the port wing just barely touched the ground. I guess it ripped loose the fuel tanks because that aircraft exploded in front of me! When it hit the ground, it exploded a second time. There wasn't a piece of person in that aircraft that you could have stuck in a paper bag. It just disintegrated—the airplane and all the people aboard. Because I was an eyewitness, I had to go before an Air Force inquiry board to detail what I saw. The thing that burned in my memory the most was that the pilot still hadn't closed the little sliding window near his head. It was still open and I could still see that fellow with his naval cap and earphones over his ears. He was just a tenth of a second from meeting his maker at that point. As long as I live I'll never forget the confident look on his face not knowing he was about to die.

HAULING COAL

Because the fairly stable duty hours I had continued, I was able to work several other part-time jobs. I was a married man now and needed more income to support my wife. At this time, I was on night duty, and I had my days free. Night duty involved several shifts. We operated the motor pool twenty-four hours a day. It was around the clock because the war went on twenty-four hours a day. There was no such thing as a period of rest because of the military need. While night duty wasn't quite as hectic as daytime duty, I still went out quite a bit. I had my share of driving at night through both the second and the third shifts, which took me through to breakfast. It was during this time that I accepted a part-time job driving a truck for a coal company during my off duty hours. At the time I took the job I was working third shift, eleven at night until seven in the morning. I would eat breakfast and then go to my part-time job. One of my duties was to load coal into twenty-five and fifty pound bags. Coal was sold that way in the communities where people could only afford or store small quantities of coal at a time. It was dusty, dirty work but it was all right. All in all, it was no hardship.

I worked out well enough in the coal company. One day the boss asked me if I could drive a truckload of coal and put it into a cellar in the commercial district somewhere in Washington. I had never driven a coal truck with a hydraulic lift before, so I didn't know much about how it worked. I was a little bit too embarrassed to ask and quite frankly, there was no one else working there except the boss. So, off I went! I was to go to a storefront that was opposite a trolley-loading platform. There were double tracks in the street and the trolley-loading platform occupied the center between the tracks. The tracks were a little bit close to the curbside. I had to occupy those tracks in order to put the chute in the basement manhole. Then I had to raise the bed of the truck to let the coal go down the chute into the coal bin. I thought it would only take a couple of minutes. I don't know exactly what happened, but I lost the load of coal! It went all over the trolley tracks and the sidewalk. The trolley was delayed, as it couldn't pass. Did I ever tie up the traffic in Washington! Of course, being a GI I had a hard time getting away with it. The police came, and I had to hand shovel all of the coal off the tracks and out of the road. There must have been fifteen trolley cars standing there waiting for me to finish! I felt like a jerk. Fortunately, it never got into the newspapers. Afterward, I went back, and I quit that job because I couldn't afford to jeopardize my military career. Not only did I not want to lose rank, but I also did not want to be reassigned to a less favorable job.

PACKAGE HANDLING

After I left the coal company, I got a good part-time job with the Railway Express Agency in Washington located near Union Station. Again, this job was sanctioned by my commanding officer. I was working second shift in my Army job at that time—three p.m. to eleven p.m.—because we had rotated shifts. As soon as my shift would end, I'd report to work at Railway Express, about midnight. Railway Express was very short-handed and were eager to give part-time work to GIs. They had a sorting room where things were broken down into different points for transshipment. There was a mountain of packages in there, more than I had ever seen in one place. It was a huge pile and more kept coming in with each arriving train.

There were about half a dozen of us working, and we were all service people. In addition to soldiers, there were sailors and marines. We would sort these packages and carry them to another bin for transshipment. This was a frustrating job where you never got to the bottom of the huge pile of outgoing parcels. I think the packages that were on the bottom must have been there for two months, and they were probably going to be there for another two months because we could never get to them. If anything in those packages at the bottom of the heap was perishable, it wouldn't have lasted long enough to get where it was going.

I was pretty much of a hustler. A lot of people in the military learn how to goof off. I always felt that I owed the Railway Express people a night's work because they were paying me for one. So I hustled. I guess I got noticed by one of the supervisors because he put me on a different detail which involved emptying freight cars that came in with truckloads of naval cannon powder. These canisters of powder were to go out to the Navy base in Anacostia, and I believe they were to be used in the big guns. The powder was loaded separately from the shell in those big sixteen-inch cannons. I figured they were for the large guns because the cans of powder were big and had to be hand carted.

I also recall when special shipments of paper would come in. This was the paper the government printing office used to print our currency. *Every* roll of that paper had an armed guard with it. I remember being at the off loading of the freight cars and getting the paper onto the Treasury Department trucks, where it was then transported to the printing office to be transformed into money.

AN UNEXPECTED TRIP

On the job with the Railway Express, we could empty a freight car in a reasonable amount of time and that would be it for a while. Because I worked about ten hours a day for the military and then eight hours for Railway Express, I was getting worn down and was not getting enough sleep. One night in particular, there was a caboose standing alongside the loading platform. With no train in sight to unload, I went inside it to get out of the weather and to rest my back for a few minutes. I quickly fell fast asleep. It wasn't long before I woke up because I was being rocked back and forth by the rumbling train. The caboose had been hooked up to a train and I soon realized we were headed north. It was pretty frightening. Not only was I absent from my job with Railway Express, I would soon be A.W.O.L. from the army if I went more than fifty miles or was late for duty.

Thankfully, the train got up somewhere around Bowie, Maryland near the south of Baltimore. It made a stop so I got off and found a conductor. I told him that I had fallen asleep in the caboose. I waited for his response and was happy to learn that the conductor was a kind man. I told him that I had to be back for duty in a couple of hours, and if I wasn't there, I would be A.W.O.L. and in real big trouble. I knew I wouldn't be working for the Railway Express any longer either. The conductor made arrangements with a train going back to Union Station and put me aboard it. I got back to duty on time, but I sure lost a lot of sleep that particular night.

My job at the Railway Express lasted a short while longer. It gave me an opportunity to send Margie a little extra money here and there. I think the only reason that I gave up that job was because I was sent back out to Fort Myer again. I left the C Street Barracks, which placed me too far away to come back and forth to Washington for any kind of part-time employment.

Pfc. Richard Nabbe 32920618
Ordnance Dept.
A.P.O. #7505
c/o Postmaster, N.Y.C., N.Y.

Pfc. Rob Nabbe
Motor Center Detach.
2131 "C" St. N.W.
Washington, D.C.

February 5, 1944

Dear Rob;

Just a line to let you know I received your letter at Ft. Reynolds. I'm somewhere in New England. You guess where? The weather is fine up here and it isn't bad at all. Also the chow is the best I have had in a long time. Quite unusual in the Army.

I see that you too don't receive my mail. Well Rob like I told Mom, I answer every letter as soon as I receive them. They are also mailed at the same time. Why you folks don't get them is beyond me. I'm sure I can't get them to you any quicker than the mailman will get them there. It appears that the mail system stinks from there. Mom wrote me about the same thing and I write her almost every day. You figure it out! I got a letter from Margie a couple days ago and it was quite a surprise. Please let her know I'll write her as soon as I get a chance. Right now things are pretty uncertain so I don't think it's advisable to write everyone as I'll probably be gone before I get any return mail.

If you care to, take a chance on dropping me a line.

Well Rob I can't say anymore for more reason than one so I will just say so long for now.[12]

Be good and keep working on that film if you can.

As ever,

Your Brother
Rich

---

12 The front of this letter has a stamp that says, "PASSED BY U 105 05 Army Examiner" with a signature (undecipherable).

Pfc. Richard Nabbe 32920618[13]
Ord. Dep't. A. P. O. 7505
c/o Postmaster, N.Y.C., N.Y.

Pfc. Robert Nabbe
Motor Center Detach.
2131 "C" St. "N.W."
Washington, D.C.

March 15, 1944

Dear Rob,

Well Rob, I hope you got my V-mail letter O.K. As it's the fastest method of mail I buzzed one or two right off. I'm making time to get you this letter off to you. I received two V-mail letters from you today. Thanks a lot for writing, its sure swell of you to write even if you don't get an answer right away. It's not my fault though, we wish we could get a dozen a day off to you folks but we have very little time right now. [14]
Subject: Weather
The weather stinks here. It is damp as hell and it takes about 3 or 4 days to dry a pair of sox. They say you can get used to it in time, but I don't expect to stay her for fifty years. Our pet rib to the limeys is that we are going to cut these barrage balloons loose and let this damned place sink. I actually believe they hold this place up.

We are really getting some rugged training. [Part of letter cut out by censor]. I should be in good shape by the time we get through. That is "if" we ever get through. We are just casuals[15] *waiting to be assigned to a company and we may leave here in a week or maybe 6 months. Boy each night I say a prayer that I leave here soon. The food is pretty good but we have a hell of a time getting enough most of the time. They sure are fussy about the outgoing of food here and I can't say that I blame 'em much.*

I have been to a couple English towns and cities and there is very little to do except

---

13   The front of the envelope has a stamped orange airplane in a circle surrounded by the words "U.S. POSTAGE VIA AIR MAIL". It also has a censor's stamp "Processed by 33968 Army Examiner" and is signed "W. I. Huddleston 2nd Lt." There also is a red stamped circle around the words "PASSED BY BASE 1070 ARMY EXAMINER" and the letters "US" are on either side of the 1070.

14   There is a hole in the letter in paragraph 2. An army censor physically removed the portion.

15   A casual was a *soldier* temporarily attached to a unit while awaiting permanent assignment.

drink 0.0 beer in pubs. Oy! What lousy stuff! It's warm and bitter and it tastes lousy! Give me good old American beer any old day. The women you can give back to the Indians, I'll stick to good American gals exclusively. Please give my regards to the females in Washington. I'd like to be back with 'em! I would sure like to be with you when you are fishing. That's some size catfish you are catching. If there is any of my fishing tackle home you can use, you are welcome to it. I won't need them for a long time. Mom says grandpa is pretty sick. I hope he pulls out all right.

How is Margie doing? All right I guess! Well Bob that's about all for now as I must get some sleep to make another hike tomorrow. Pray you stay in Washington because you'll be sorry if you leave. If you think there is too much chicken-shit where you are, just hop a boat and come over here. Just bring a divers suit along. You'll need it. Well Rob that's all for now so I'll say so long for a while and I'll write again soon. Thanks again and regards to Margie.

Your Brother
Rich

P.F.C. Richard Nabbe
ORD. DEPT., A.P.O. 7505
c/o Postmaster, N.Y.C., N.Y.

Pfc. Robert Nabbe
Motor Center Detach.
2131 "C" St. N.W.
Washington, D.C.

March 29,1944

Dear Rob;

*Just a line to let you know how things are going in the dear old E.T.O[16]. Ah,
what a lovely day it isn't today! I swear if I was scheduled to be shot at sunrise, I would
be able to survive for at least six months excluding all accidents pertaining to weather
conditions. I guess you can draw your own conclusions old boy. Also, when I took my last
receding look at the vanishing shores of the U.S.A., I says to myself, "there goes all my
chicken shit with my beloved homeland." Yeah! We were just issued divers suits and you
don't need an imagination what for. Let's just hope the pressure doesn't get to great or
we'll need a divers bell. Well Rob, we must put up with those little things.*

*We are really getting quite a bit of training here Rob and I must say that most of
it is really interesting. So far we have disassembled the 50 & 30 cal. Machine gun; the
carbine and M. rifle; hand grenades, hand to hand combat and any other number of
useful field training topics. I guess there aren't many subjects they have left out. We get a
bit of every branch of the service for some reason. Almost every day we go on a hike, so
my legs are getting pretty tough. Some of those babys we go on are really bad though and
I wonder how I'll hold up at times.*

*The towns aren't bad about here but there isn't much to do. We drink English beer
and some of the stuff isn't too bad. Liquor is like finding oil in New Jersey.*

---

16   E. T. O. stands for European Theater of Operations. The term "theater of
     operations" was defined in the U.S. Army field manuals as "the land and sea areas to
     be invaded or defended, including areas necessary for administrative activities incident
     to the military operations". It referred to Army Ground Forces, United States Army
     Air Forces, and Army Service Forces operations north of Italy and the Mediterranean
     coast, in the European Theatre of World War II. It was bordered to the south by the
     North African Theater of Operations, US Army (NATOUSA), which later became
     the Mediterranean Theater of Operations (MTOUSA).

It seems like shoe leather is hard to find for civilians so the kids all have wooden soles on their shoes. Most of them go so far as to put sheet metal on the soles. Result! When you go marching down the street you get the illusion that the light Calvary is coming at you. But don't be afraid, old boy, it's only a flock of kids ready to mob you. First thing, a couple of iron shodden kids run up to you and start their usual line of questions such as "ya got any gum, ya got any cigarettes, candy, cigars or etc." I swear they would take the buttons off your blouse if they could. Well now, you're a rookie and you have a spare slice of gum in your pocket so you start to look for it. Well Rob that's your worse mistake you ever made in your life. All of a sudden about 90 kids appear out of no where and they climb all over you. Now you are the Pied Piper # 2 without a flute. My god it's murder. Result, you merely say, no gum, no nothing, the next time a couple approach you. If more than two corner you, you run like hell and hope you can lose 'em. My gosh what a war will do to people. The people pay an awful price for cigarettes and they stink. When we have any cigarettes to spare, we give them to the English folks. They only cost us 4 1/2 cents a pack over here. The trouble is though, we only get seven packs a week. Can't be too generous at that rate. Great place England. I'm afraid I can't pass judgment as yet because I haven't seen too much to form an opinion as yet.

You know Rob, the water system is kind of sad here. It seems that it lacks minerals or something but anyhow it reacts on you like beer does. You drink it and after awhile you have to drain your crankcase. Now I mean you either get rid of it or you change your underwear. Almost all the guys are affected by it so you see it's not us. The same goes for other things too!! Now English beer is slightly different. That keeps you going constantly and that no lie. I doubt if I have any kidneys anymore. I must just have a straight hose running clear through me. I have a new game now. It's a race to see if I can get my shoes on and down to the latrine before I drizzle in my long johns. This goes on all night, seven days a week. Quite a lot of exercise. Seeing how clothes are so hard to keep clean here, I'm seriously thinking of going to bed with a milk bottle.

They are quite liberal on details around here too. We are constantly on K.P. or guard duty all the time. Oh For the life of a casual! Phoooey. Getting back to the women, it seems they have a definite lack of calcium in their diet and they have little or no teeth. My gosh you should see some of these babes. Pretty as a picture till they smile. Its not odd at all to see young chickens with false teeth. It's really a shame.

I'll give the army this much credit though, they really have pretty good food. Our chow lines are a mile long for chow but it only takes about an hour to get through it so you see it's not so bad.

I'll put a line of sympathy in here for the censor because he probably will tear his hair out after reading all this. I'd also like to apologize for writing on both sides of the paper, but as I am at a definite shortage on paper I'm sure he'll understand.

  Well Rob, this is about all I can think of at present (thank God) so I'll say good bye. I still read your previous letters and I still get quite a kick out of them.

  Bye now and be good. If you write me write me air mail.

  Your brother,
   Rich

SCRUBBING FLOORS AGAIN

By this time I reoccupied the Pentagon Garage, which had two levels with an enormous amount of floor area. Every morning the garage floor was scrubbed immaculately clean. We used mineral spirits, about a drum of it a day. The fluid was sprinkled on the garage floor with watering cans and all of the available personnel had to get brooms. An announcement over the loudspeaker would call out, "Sweepers, man your brooms." That meant that we had to scrub the entire garage to remove the minutest traces of oil drippings left by any of the vehicles. It was a job none of us enjoyed but had to be done.

The military was pretty clean about things. Plus, this was a way to keep everybody's time occupied productively. After the floor was scrubbed, high-pressure hoses were used to flush off the dirty mineral spirits into drains. I guess that it went into the Potomac River eventually. Today, of course, it wouldn't be permitted. But back in those days, it was the way things were done. After all these many years any time I smell mineral spirits, I instantly hear a little voice in my subconscious saying, "Sweepers, man your brooms."

MOVED AGAIN

About that time, the Women's Army Corp was trained and the Army began putting the women into jobs that would release men for combat. That happened to us. The men were all transferred to some other point. The women came in, and the men were reassigned to other places. I was sent to another army camp. I don't recall the name or where it was located but it was a port of embarkation. After processing a soldier was put on a boat to be shipped to his new destination. I had no idea where I was being sent or what my new assignment would be. It crossed my mind that I might be sent overseas.

BACK TO THE PENTAGON GARAGE

After I had been there for a few days, I was called into the orderly room one morning. Of course, here I was again, one of ten million guys and how do they know me? I didn't do anything spectacular and I didn't do anything wrong, so I was rather amazed to have my name called out to report to the orderly room. As it turned out, three of us were taken from our outfit and returned to the Pentagon Garage. This posed a real strange situation. There were one hundred forty W.A.C.s who had been brought in to take care of the duties that the men had been doing. Then we three guys were temporarily brought back until we could be replaced. We were eventually to rejoin our outfit. I later learned that everybody else from our outfit was sent to Germany to the European theater. I barely missed going overseas to face battle.

In the Women's Army Corp there were non-commissioned officers and women officers. There was one lone male in the Pentagon Garage and that was Captain Kelly. At one time he had been one of my commanding officers. Here we were, four men with one hundred-forty women. It was quite an arrangement. Captain Kelly was about as unhappy about the duty as we were. It wasn't that I disliked the women; I just didn't want to serve with women officers telling me what to do. In any event, I went in and said to the captain that I certainly wasn't anxious to go into combat and get shot, but at the same time I wasn't too happy with this arrangement. I asked, "When am I going to catch up with my outfit?" He responded, "Well, you're here temporarily for several weeks, two weeks maybe three."

The rationale for our being there was that there were some duties the army would not permit the women to perform. One was going on overnight trips with officers, as I was accustomed to doing. They also wouldn't allow the women to use the motorcycles for whatever reason.

Over time I befriended some of the women. They were nice kids, and I liked most of them. There was one in particular that I remember. Her brother was killed in combat, and she joined the army to take his place. I guess her reason was more patriotic than many. A lot of these women were adventure seekers, and new opportunities were now open to them. Taking advantage of the military's needs for the war effort, women enlisted to serve their country while also procuring meaningful work.

I do remember one ritual. This is before today's awareness of sexually transmitted diseases and AIDS. When the paymaster would come in, he'd issue condoms to everybody. There were only three of us enlisted men, but he would issue condoms to all the women, too. The women were instructed to use them. I believe this was more to prevent the pregnancies because pregnancy is more expensive for the military than treating venereal diseases.

SHARING FACILITIES

One little issue that was always awkward for the men was that the motor pool garage in the Pentagon building was set up strictly for males. There were no female restrooms so the latrine was allocated to us four men from ten minutes before the hour to the hour, every hour. I guess the women, particularly after having been out driving around a bit, had to use the facility. They would come in, forgetting that these ten minutes were allocated to the guys. I'd be in the latrine and here would come a couple of women busting in. It was always an embarrassing encounter. Most of the facilities were male urinals. There were a limited number of conventional toilets, so there was always a long line of women awaiting their turns. The point was that we never did get our ten minutes of privacy. I don't imagine there was once that I was in there during my allocated time when I wasn't interrupted. But, eventually, I got used to that too.

WAR & NAVY
DEPARTMENTS
V-MAIL SERVICE[17]
OFFICIAL BUSINESS

Pfc. Robert Nabbe
South post, Ft. Meyer
VIRGINIA

April 1, 1944

Dear Rob,

Received a letter from mom today and she confirms your suspected theory that you were going to become a papa. Well congratulations to you old boy. I know that you and Marge are really happy about the whole thing. By the time I get around to getting hitched, I guess I'll be old enough to retire as a bachelor. Well maybe I'm better off because by the looks of things here I'll be a nervous wreck and not fit to live with anyway. How are things going with you back home? I haven't heard from you in some time now. I've written you quite a few letters and V-mails. By now you should have gotten some word from me. Well Rob that all for now. Bye

> *Your Brother*
> *Rich*

---

17   This letter was sent via V-MAIL. It is tiny—5" x 4.25". V-MAIL had to be folded
     in a special way so that the recipient's name and address showed through the small
     window on the front of the envelope.

*WAR & NAVY
DEPARTMENTS
V-MAIL SERVICE
OFFICIAL BUSINESS*

*Pfc. Robert Nabbe
South post, Ft. Meyer
VIRGINIA*

April 6, 1944

Dear Rob;

I'm sorry as hell you aren't getting my mail. I write you enough, you should receive some. I did put one part of stupidity on your mail and that was writing your old address on all your mail. I swear I never thought to look and see that you had moved. In all instances that's probably why you aren't getting mail very well. What a brain, eh? I read in "Stars and Stripes" that you folks have had quite a bit of snow back home. Cheer up lad, spring is just around the corner. It's about time you caught a fish down there. What's the matter, aren't you putting any bait on the hook? Maybe you were trying to beat the season. Things are just about the same, Rob. It rains every day and its' real nice and muddy. Ah me such lovely weather. Well "daddy" I must get dressed for war. So be good.

"Uncle Rich"

*WAR & NAVY
DEPARTMENTS
V-MAIL SERVICE
OFFICIAL BUSINESS*

*Pfc. Robert Nabbe
South Post, Ft. Meyer
Virginia*

April 10, 1944

Dear Rob;

I've dropped you quite a few letters but I guess you aren't getting them. Let's hope I have more luck on this one. I received a letter from Bourke[18] over here. Maybe I'll get a chance to see him. I have taken a few pictures with my camera but I need film. I don't suppose there is much sense in asking you for any because you had such a time before. I'll just have to do the best I can over here. I figure I'll have quite a few interesting pictures when I do get back home. Well, daddy, I guess by now the fish are biting in the Olde Potomac. I wish I was there with you old boy. Easter was quite uneventful over here. Of course I dazzled the population with my new shoe laces. Quite a dud I am. Well Rob, give my love to Margie and I'll write again soon.

*Your Bud
Rich*

---

18   Fred Bourke was a friend of Richard's from his home in Irvington, New Jersey, Fred's father had a cleaning and pressing shop in the neighborhood. Robert says, "I never cared for the chap, but he was Richard's friend who also would up overseas in the army during World War II. I wasn't aware that he was drafted as it happened after my own inductment [sic] into the army."

Pfc. Richard Nabbe – 32920618
Ord Dep't A.P.O. 6505
c/o Post Master, N.Y., N.Y.

Pfc. Robert Nabbe
South Post, Fort Meyer
Virginia

April 20, 1944

Dear Rob:

Received your letter of April 2, and believe me bub, I was sure glad to hear from you. I haven't had mail for quite some time and I'm glad to hear from you. I suppose it's silly to keep harping on the subject but I hope your patience hasn't reached a very low ebb pertaining to my mail to you. Just trust the fact that I have no intentions of forgetting you and that sooner or later you will get all the mail I have written to you. It's a miserably slow process Rob but as I say, just have faith and I'm sure you'll get all the information you'd like to know. I have received quite a lot of mail from you so you can rest assured that your efforts have not been in vain or unappreciated.

Rob, this page had to be written over because the censor sent back the letter with a note saying I violated a censorship rule. Now I'm not saying the censor is wrong but I read the paragraph in question over quite a few times and I can't see anything of any military value to anyone in it. I guess I'll just have to stick to the weather and hope the sun shines for a day so I could change the subject.

To revert to a few subjects on the previous page, I mentioned that it's getting to be quite like spring here. Leaves are popping out and it gets nice and warm when the sun comes out. It rains pretty near every day here, so I just take it for granted that its monsoon weather. I pray to god to send me back to Jersey via air mail.

I also mentioned something about the training but as I stated before its snafu[19]. So back to the weather! Surprise!! I got a letter from Herbie[20] today! What a goon he is. He's had a bit of hard luck with his hand but is O.K. now! The next page you will have to figure out for yourself so —

Well Rob, don't get the idea that I'm on the verge of taking a brody or something. Even though it has entered my mind, I wouldn't give them the satisfaction of pinning

---

19   Translation: situation normal: all f***ed up
20   Herbie Hertlein, his childhood friend.

anything on me. Also I have all intentions of getting home as quick as I can.

I'm going to ask Ma to get me a watch. No kidding Rob I need one bad. I never missed it so much as I do here. If you can pick one up in a hock shop, it sure would help. I've tried to buy one over here but it costs a fortune. If you do run across one, I'd gladly send you a money order for it at any time. I realized that I make a pretty damned nuisance of myself Rob, but I'm sure that you realize I wouldn't think of bothering you if I thought I didn't have a sufficient reason to do so.

Well Rob, I guess you had enough sad talk for one session so I'll say good-bye. Let's hope by now that your luck has changed and you have caught a big fish. I still wish I were with you.

Your brother
Rich

STAYING PUT

The several weeks that we were supposed to be at the Pentagon Garage dragged on and on, and I never did get to rejoin my outfit. I guess that was just as well. The prospect of getting killed wasn't exactly thrilling to me, particularly since I had a bride at home. With the military you never had a choice where you were assigned. Whatever you did, it was what the army wanted you to do not what *you* wanted to do.

Eventually they did bring back men to the Pentagon Garage, for some reason. The women did a tremendous job, and there was no problem with their performance. It was excellent. But, the army brought in a whole bunch of guys, and they filled out the outfit to where it was about one hundred women and about one hundred men. It put the situation back into balance.

Everybody did fine; there were no problems. I guess there was dating amongst the single guys and the women, but as a married man I paid no attention. For the most part, I enjoyed the friendship of several of the women. It was a very friendly, one-on-one relationship. There were many nice women, and I liked a number them. More than once they loaned me the money to get home to see my wife. The women were most generous about things like that because they were quite sentimental. Ultimately, the army did get the restroom facilities straightened out, as they added another whole series of plumbing. Then the men had their restroom and the women had theirs. Problem solved.

THE DRUNKEN INDIAN

I guess because I interacted so well with the women and wasn't a threat to anybody (being a married man) I was called in to see the commanding officer one day. I was sent to the W.A.C.'s barracks. It seemed that one of the W.A.C.s was a full-blooded Indian who had gotten drunk. She had gone on the warpath, as Indians are famous for doing when they get tied in with alcohol. She was a mess. She was destroying things, and they couldn't get her out of the W.A.C.'s barracks, so they sent me up there. I'm not a diplomat, and I just couldn't understand why I was selected. Why didn't they send in

M.P.s? Why me? They thought that I could go up there and talk her out of her war bonnet and get her back to where she could be punished. In the Army when you are given a direct order, you do it.

I went up to the barracks and tried to use a little reason. I said, "You know, this is most awkward for me. I shouldn't even be here. This is off-limits to men. I feel strange about it. Give me a break and come with me and just get me off the hook." That actually worked. She became very docile, very passive, and came with me. I took her and put her in the car and brought her back down to the Pentagon Garage where the officers took over. That was all I had to do about it. I tried a gentle approach, and it worked.

THE DEAD COLONEL

When the Women's Army Corp replaced the male personnel in the Motor Center Detachment, they very efficiently took over just about every function the men had performed with one or two exceptions. One in particular was manning the ambulance. I was staying in the barracks one evening in South Post, Fort Myer where I had been reassigned from the "C Street Barracks" in Washington, D.C. when I received a phone call from the W.A.C. sergeant on night duty at the Pentagon Garage. The call was to see if I could handle an ambulance assignment. I was informed that an officer had dropped dead in one of the Pentagon corridors. It was about nine or ten o'clock at night, and most of the GIs were still out carousing. I found another man who was "in for the night" to give me a hand. Presently, a staff car arrived—the Pentagon was a substantial distance from the base—and we were driven to the garage where the ambulance was parked.

The Pentagon is a huge multi-storied building with miles of corridors. I had a red badge that allowed me access to certain parts of the building. Most areas, the more sensitive sections, required badges of other colors and the officer was in one of these. It took me quite a time to obtain all the required clearances to reach the corridor where the officer laid spread eagle on his back. The deceased was a full "bird colonel" that had been lying there for some time because of the late hour, but the body was still free of rigor mortis. In life the deceased was a tall, distinguished man of large build. In death he was very limp and difficult to handle. It took the two of us some time to place him on the gurney and to roll him through the maze of corridors to the ambulance. It amazed me as to the indifference of those we passed in the building. My companion left me and returned to the barracks so I was left alone with the Colonel. I had no instructions from anyone because there had been no officer in charge, just an officer with a non-commissioned rating, who had left it up to me. He was apparently glad to be relieved of any more responsibility for the deceased. I attribute this to the late hour when much of the Pentagon was closed down. During the daytime, it was a beehive of activity including a multitude of assorted medical facilities that would normally have dealt with the situation.

I thought the only solution would be to take the colonel to the Walter Reed Hospital, which was quite a few miles outside the city. I drove him there and pulled up to the emergency room where I located a sergeant on duty. By this time, it was around midnight and very quiet. I said, "Sergeant, I have a dead officer in the ambulance. I'm bringing him here to place in your hands." The sergeant said that he didn't have any instructions for handling a body. I said, "What do you suggest?" He responded, "You'll have to do something else with him." Growing frustrated I said, "Now look, I have no place to put him. I was instructed to move him somewhere and this was the only 'somewhere' I could think of that could handle it." The sergeant asked, "Do you have a death certificate?" I said, "No, the guy just dropped dead, apparently, in a corridor in the Pentagon building. I was asked to remove him, and here he is." Refusing, the sergeant said, "I can't take him." By now I was quite upset. I glared at the sergeant and in my most assertive voice said, "Well, Sergeant, when you get out here in the morning, bright and early, and look on your lawn, you're going to see a dead colonel, 'cause he's yours." With that I guess he figured he'd better do something because he did take the colonel off my hands. By the time I got back to the Pentagon Garage with the ambulance, it must have been about two or three in the morning. I got only a few hours sleep that night.

THE NEW PLYMOUTH

I remember another incident when we "salvaged" a worn out sedan. "Salvaged" was an army term for replacing vehicles. Most of the vehicles in the garage were Chevrolet or Plymouth sedans of pre-World War II models. I guess the government snapped up for military use all the new cars that were manufactured. When they had about sixty thousand miles on them, the vehicles were considered worn out or ready to be salvaged. Each car probably had been rebuilt at least once but had reached the point of no longer being serviceable. Of course, they were in constant use, twelve hours a duty tour, day and night, and were always in motion.

Two of us took the sedan and another car to the salvage quartermaster depot to trade them in. We had driven two vehicles to pick up one. It was in the winter. I remember that well because the icy roads had a direct effect on what happened. After we dropped off the salvaged vehicles we had picked up a brand new Plymouth sedan with only twenty miles on the odometer. It had just been painted olive drab, and the numbers and military designations had been installed. On the return trip I was a passenger in the new car and the other fellow was driving.

We were returning to the Pentagon motor pool garage from the quartermaster depot, which was a number of miles out in the country. Two officers, who wanted to be returned to the Pentagon from the depot, were also passengers. We approached the city and were coming off the highway into the outskirts of Washington when we approached a traffic circle that had iced up. As we entered this traffic circle, a big Greyhound bus ahead of us went completely out of control. It whipped around in such a way that it was pivoting on its front wheels. I would say, as an analogy, that we were a baseball and it was a baseball bat as it came around and hit us—I mean demolished us.

As a front seat passenger I saw what was about to happen so I threw myself down on the floorboards just in time. The last thing that I saw was the hood and all the rest of the car going up in the air over the windshield. Then I was crushed down into this tiny little space with the rear of the seat and the two officers in the back wedged on top of me. The driver was crushed up against the steering wheel.

With all of that weight on me, I could hardly breathe. I thought I was going to die. I really thought I was going to die. I was covered with blood, and I just couldn't breathe at all. I actually feared that I would suffocate. Help appeared quickly and the mangled doors were finally dragged apart by the military police. They pulled us out and laid us in the snow bank. I sensed that I was, for the most part, uninjured, but I was the only one that was. The officers were badly hurt, and the driver was a mess. He had spokes from the steering wheel through his lower jaw and fragments of shattered glass all through his face. His ribs were broken.

We were lying there in the snow where the M.P.s had laid us. Because we had driven up to the depot and the car was heated, I hadn't even put on my overcoat. I was freezing to death and kept trying to get up, but an M.P. kept pushing me down. He said, "You have to lay there. You're hurt." And I said, "No, I'm not." He responded, "You are, too. The ambulances are on the way and you are not supposed to move." I said, "Well, I'm freezing to death here, and I'm going to get up anyhow." So I pushed myself to my feet and just about that time, the ambulances came and loaded us all up. They got us to the hospital where they took my clothes off to examine me all over. I had some scrapes and bruises and contusions. Even though I was a bloody mess, it turned out that none of it was my blood. It all belonged to the other guys. I was sore for about a week, but I think the greater loss was the fact that our brand new vehicle was totally smashed beyond any salvage at all—any use left being only for spare parts.

Pfc. Richard Nabbe – 32920618
Ord. Dep't. A.P.O. 7505
c/o Postmaster, N.Y.C., N.Y.

Pfc. Robert Nabbe
South Post, Fort Meyer
Virginia

May 4, 1944

Dear Robbie,

I started a letter to you a couple days ago but we have been so damned busy, I couldn't finish it. So now I start anew and will finish this if it takes all nite. I just came off of K.P. so if a yawn starts once in awhile, don't be alarmed. Rob, I know how disappointing it is not to receive mail, but I'm having a hell of a time of it and I can't get them off as I like. For three weeks I got one letter and in the last three days I got about thirty some. From previous letters you can probably see that censorship is really pretty strict, so if I can't answer a letter I'm simply lost for a topic of conversation. I did receive a nice long air mail letter from you and it's from that, that this is based upon.

I guess it's up with grandpa[21], Rob, so its no use of hoping anymore. Poor old guy sure has had a tough time of it. May God be with him.

I'm sorry Margie is sick. By now I pray she feels much better. Tell her to take care of herself will you. We have enough trouble of our own without her being on sick call.

You seem to be having quite a time with the weather. Well it's quite the same here with the exception that we don't have no snow. It's a lot like late spring here. Everything is in pretty near full bloom also.

I was driving a six by six truck[22] one day this week. Well it's my first time and I'm rather green at it. The driver and me was having a heated discussion about double clutching when a nice big red cow strolls lazily in front of ye olde vehicle. Boy I could see the steaks frying right before my eyes. Well the driver had a different idea about the steaks and he starts going into hysterics. I slapped the brakes on hard and the truck stood up on her non directionals. We missed old bossy by a hair on her tail, but I compacted twelve guys in the truck into a space wide as a deck of cards. You should hear

---

21 Richard and Robert's grandfather, Herman Gottfried Koelsch
22 A six by six truck is an army transport vehicle for personnel and freight. It had two
     front wheels and four back wheels for heavy loads.

those guys yell phrases of discontentment. What an awful cussing! Well the driver put his transmission together and kicked me out of the cab. Now all I had to do was crawl into a mess of squashed GI's in the back. Oh how I ever retain my original shape is beyond me. Sometimes I think American sportsmanship isn't so hot. Ah, but life is so interesting at times. Burrrp!

I got a letter from Jimmy H[23]. today and I never thought a person could sound so disgusted. I don't blame the poor guy though. He even went so far as to get married. I think he's off his nut! Poor J. H. is all shot to hell. I guess that cutting oil is getting under his skin. (ugh!)

Wal fisherman, I'm dying for a bit of shut eye so I'll end here. Let me know how the fish are running and I'll tell you what bait to use.

Give my regards to the little woman and remember that when the bullets are flying like Jersey mosquitoes, I'll wish you were here with me. After all you are bigger than me by a pound or two and I do need some protection. (I'm only kidding!)

I'll write again soon as I get a chance.

"Sob"
Your brother
Rich[24]

---

23   Jimmy H. is James Horahan, a family friend. Because of a physical deformity he was not drafted. Jimmy worked as a screw machine operator that sprayed a continuous stream of cutting oil on the part being machined.

24   Handwritten on the back of this letter is a note from Robert to his wife, Marjorie: "Honey—please save this letter for me as I keep all Richie's mail."

Pfc. Richard Nabbe -32920618
Ord. Dep't. A.P.O. 7505
c/o Postmaster, N.Y.C. N.Y.

Pfc. Robert Nabbe
South Post, Fort Meyer
Virginia
"C" St.

May 5, 1944

Dear Rob,

Well old boy I received two air mail letters from you today. I swear I don't know how you do it but the receiver really enjoys them very much. I also got a very nice letter from Margy too. I was surprised to hear from her but it was really nice of her I think.

Say, you are having quite a bit of financial difficulty aren't you? With junior on his way I don't doubt it.[25] I'll tell you what I'll do. I get more money than I need here so I'll send you a few bucks as soon as I can get down to the post office. We don't get much of a chance to spend our money so we only gamble it away anyhow. Maybe you'll get a little fun out of it. It won't do you any good to argue with me because I'm way over here and you are way over there. Ha! Ha! Just don't tell Margie or she'll raise hell. Next letter old boy! Besides its worth a couple of bucks to get mail from you.

How the hell do you get in so much trouble? No kidding, Rob if you ain't always falling in the damned Potomac River you wind up bopping a general in the can with a car door.[26] I'm sure if you led my miserable existence you would be damned glad to be in Washington where something happens once in a while.

Hey! It isn't the battery that's cheap in that Packard, it's ye old radio. You ain't kidding anybody, bub, you know as well as I do what runs it down. I think you have seven points to your section eight already.[27] Youze is a screw ball.

---

25   Richard refers to the impending birth of Robert and Marjorie's first child, Susan Carol Nabbe, born October 18, 1944.

26   Robert states, "I don't remember what he's talking about me falling into the Potomac River. I used to swim in it during the summer when Washington was hot. As for the general, I saluted the general as he exited as required and slammed the door to the car just as the general reached back in to get something off the front seat. Luckily, I didn't get into trouble."

27   Richard refers to "section eight". The term to a category of discharge from the United States military for reason of being mentally unfit for service. The term comes

Say Rob, that vision you painted of your new home is really swell. However, regardless of how nice it is of you and Marge to think of me like that, you know I don't want you to do anything like that for me. When you two get a home, you'll be damned glad I ain't haunting hell out of you. Besides you'll need all the rooms you can get for that flock of kids you are raising. As far as ducking bullets goes, I don't know if I can out duck any, but I'll sure as hell stay hid deep enough so they'll have to do some fancy shooting to plug me. (I hope) Maybe I'll catch a few scalps myself. Rob, I hope you won't feel offended by what I said about your home. All I want you to know is that I wouldn't want to cause an imposition on you folks for the world. You and Marge are the swellest people I know and before I'd even think of causing any difficulties among us, well, anyway you weren't kidding about catching up on fun. We have a lot of beer drinking to catch up with and also lots of hikes and fishing. Just as soon as we kick hell out of Adolph, I'll come floating back to the gold ole USA. Yipeeeeee.

You know, I feel foolish trying to write you a nice long letter so I can equal one of yours. Damned, but I wish I could write you something for a change. Oh well this will have to do for the present. I'll slip you a couple of V mails[28] in between so you know I don't forget you entirely.

My poor drooping lids are really heavy Rob so I'll close for a bit. Take care of yourself "Daddy" and I'll write again very soon.

Your brother
   "Unk" Rich

PS Go easy on your poor back!

---

from Section VIII of the World War II-era United States Army Regulation 615-360, which provided for the discharge of those deemed unfit for military service.

28 V-MAIL stands for Victory Mail. It was a system for delivering mail between those at home in the United States and troops serving abroad during World War II. V-mail correspondence worked by photographing large amounts of censored mail reduced to thumbnail size onto reels of microfilm, which weighed much less than the original would have. The film reels were shipped by priority air freight (when possible) to the US, sent to prescribed destinations for enlarging at a receiving station near the recipient, and printed out on lightweight photo paper. These facsimiles of the letter-sheets were reproduced about one-quarter the original size and the miniature mail was delivered to the addressee.

Pfc. Richard Nabbe -32920618
Ord. Dep't. A.P.O. 7505
c/o Post Master, N.Y.C., N.Y.

Pfc Robert Nabbe
Motor Center Detachment
South Post Fort Meyer
Virginia

May 26, 1944

Greetings Rob!

From dear old Camp "prostitute". I suppose you'd like to know how it got that name? Well the truth is that we have been intercoursed so regularly around here that we have to take a "pro" – twice a day to keep our morale up. (Note censor: The above is copywrited). Oh! Woe to the Joe[29] in the ETO! It's really not that bad Rob, but the life of a casual is terrible. Ah! What a future I have in store for me. Just keep saving all the corks you can find because I'll probably need them.[30] That will probably be the only way I'll hold water after awhile.

Enough of this gruesome chatter, let's be on a more cheerful subject. How are you making out? Mom says you will be where you are for quite awhile yet. Yeah! That's fine old boy. I hope you stay there for the duration. I'm sure you would never enjoy it over here half as much as you do there. Even if you don't like it.

I haven't heard from you in quite a while now, and I haven't much to say except answer what I receive from you. It's really tough old boy!

Say, how do you like our kid sister taking off to Kentucky? I hope she has fun. It's about time she got around a bit, don't you think?

I just sent some films to the signal corps to be developed and censored. If they ever come back, I'll send them along. Pictures have to be censored so they can make sure they don't contain military information. Takes time you know?

I received a letter from Herbie and is he having trouble. It seems Ruthie[31] is having her bundle of joy a little early and old Herbie has chewed all his finger nails plus his toe nails off in anxiety. (How are you sweating lately?) The baby will probably survive. The

---

29   Joe refers to G. I. Joe, the nickname of the American soldier
30   "Save all the corks" refers to Richard's fear of being shot full of holes by the enemy.
31   Ruth Hertlein, Herbie's wife.

question is, will Herb?

I got in touch with Bob Kless[32] here, but I doubt if I'll be able to meet him. Passes are scarcer here than feathers on Sally Rand's fan, so you can see why.

Well Rob that's all for now so I'll climb into my nice hard fart sock so I can endure tomorrows perils. Give my regards to Margie and keep punching (and not what you think!)

Write soon please!!
Your calloused casual brother
Richy

---

32   Bob Kless was a neighbor back home in Irvington. Robert says, "His mother babied him so much (only child) most of us kids didn't care for him but Richard took a liking to him and became involved for whatever reason—maybe pity? I never thought he would have been drafted, as he was effeminate as was Bob Mitchell next door to us who always played dolls with Dorothy.

Pfc. Richard Nabbe
32920618
Ord. Dep't. A.P.O. 7505
c/o Post Master, N.Y.C., N.Y.

Pfc. Robert Nabbe
32598454
M.C.D. 2525 S.U.
S. Post, Ft Meyer,
Virginia

May 31, 1944

Dear Rob,

Please accept my apologies old boy for doubting for a minute your sincerity about writing. Of all people, I know damned well you wouldn't fail me. The truth of the matter is, that I have moved so damned many times that it takes two weeks for mail to reach me after it gets to England. You should see the envelopes. They are so marked up from being bounced around, that I can hardly make out the name on it. Yesterday, I received twenty nine letters in a bunch. Three air mails were yours and also a couple of V-mails. Believe me, Rob, I had a swell time reading them too. We are restricted to camp most all the time, so you can see when I received all those letters, I was in heaven. If it wasn't for mail, I'd really go completely nuts. Just to give you an idea as to what goes on, we had three field inspections here in the last three days and to-morrow we have another one on full field packs. We waited about nine hours out in the hot sun to-day just waiting for the colonel to breeze by without even looking at the damned display. If you call that fun, I'll go to hell. This place really has me down. I was never so disgusted with the whole army as I am here. We can't even leave the camp to go to the Red Cross. I feel like a prisoner of war. Don't feel bad about your job, Rob. I'd take it with no pay at all right now. Boy you haven't seen anything of the army yet and I hope you never do. No use bitching because I came this far and I guess I'll have to go right on with the rest of it.

Rob, I don't know how in the hell you get into so many jams, but you sure do. I swear I laugh tell my sides hurt at those letters you write. Especially the one about that dame you had chasing you around the trolley. Wow! How do you ever do it. My gosh, you have more experiences in one day than I do in six months.

You must have lots of fun at your new job. I give you a lot of credit for having the ambition to try and get ahead. However, if you don't stop sleeping in those box cars, you'll be back in the army sleeping all night again. I can't say I'd blame you though because it sure is rough working so many hours a day and not getting enough sleep. However, I bet Margie thinks the world of you for it and you'll surely benefit from it in the long run.

I sent Mom $25 to either get me a new watch or get the old one fixed. She wrote that she is getting old one fixed up so it will do fine. You're a real pal for trying to pick me up one, Rob, I appreciate it. I know you'd do anything you could for me and I'd do the same for you. Never fear, if I need any thing, I won't hesitate to ask you. If you do get film Rob, I'll be looking for it. I pester hell out of everybody around here and I almost got a roll yesterday but he got away. I'll snag one yet.

You seem to be rolling in wealth back yonder. I guess by now you received my letter in which I stated I'd send you some dough. Believe me I can't get time to even get a money order off to you. I bet you think I'm full of bull, but I'm not. I suppose you know you don't need the few bucks now so I'll tell ya what, I'll be a whole sale welsher and won't send it, but if ever you need any money and I have it, you write and if I got it, you have my promise that you'll get it. No fooling Rob, I sincerely mean it. Old money bags Nabbe, that's me! Oh yeah!

Before I forget, thanx a million for the picture of Mom and Dad. Only you could think of that. Another mark for your efficiency old boy. Rest assured I shall take very good care of it. If you have one of you, I'll take that too. An informal one I mean! Of course I have the one of you in uniform but I'd like to have one of you in a more casual way. I'd remember you much easier that way.

I bet Margie[33] liked those pearls you bought her. She's so appreciative you know, so I'll bet she was tickled pink. Did you get to Califon?[34] Gee I bet it's swell up there now. I'd love to throw a line in that river once more. Speaking of fish, we have a stream near by and it has the biggest German trout in it. Of course, they are English property and I'm a Joe, so that fixes that. I'd have to kiss King George to even dangle a hook in their damned old river. It burns me up. Every thing that grows or swims is ward of the king. And it's like cutting your throat to ever touch them. This country is still the same as it was a hundred years ago, and I doubt if it will ever change. That is as far as tradition goes. They can keep it too! I wouldn't live over here for the Kings crown.

I was just reading over this other letter about the gold fish experience and I swear I thought I'd die. I bet you had a real time with that bunch flopping around the gutter. My

---

33   Margie, Robert's wife, was midway through her pregnancy with her first child when Richard penned this letter.

34   Califon is a place in New Jersey where Richard and Robert like to fish.

goodness what an experience. Why didn't you can them and send them as sardines? I'd eat them! As a matter of fact, I probably wouldn't know the difference.

Those chickens were also quite a mess I surmise. You should write a book on your experiences in good old Washington and you would clean up.

Well Rob, these guys are yelling for lights out, so I'll have to say so long for now. I'll drop you another line soon, so till then "adios amigo".

Your brother
"Uncle" Richie

P.S. I wish I had a girl to insult right now.

DRIVING THE OFFICERS

I continued to be part of the motor center detachment of the 2525th Service Unit. I guess it was about this time that I was assigned, more or less, to drive for General Officers and military brass in the upper ranks. I was given a new Packard sedan. It, too, was painted olive drab, but it had a shiny olive drab exterior while the rest of the vehicles were a dull military color. It was a new car, a 1941 Packard. Everything else was either a Chevrolet or Plymouth so this was quite a fancy vehicle. At the same time there was another chap who had a similar car to drive. So the two of us were then assigned to chauffeur only high-ranking officers … driving the "holy brass", we called it.

One of the officers that I drove for quite often was the head of the Women's Army Corps. She was Colonel Oveta Culp Hobby, a very charming, delightful, gracious lady. I thought the world of her. I drove her so often that she used to ask me all about my family and our new daughter, Susan. I really liked that lady. She was gracious and charming, and did her job well.

I also drove three retired generals whom I would pick up at hotels in the early morning and take to the war department building. These were retired army generals, but they had been reactivated. They were nice people. It seemed to me that most of the General Officers of the upper echelon of the military had a certain behavior about them—a certain amount of respect for the enlisted personnel. This is what I deduced after having been associated with any number of them. It's the middle range—the majors and captains and light colonels—that were a bit arrogant and snippy. But the generals, for the most part, were very, very nice to the chauffeurs. Our assignments usually were given on a daily basis but every once in a while I would be committed to one person for a period of time.

POLISHING THE BRASS

I remember one instance where I was assigned to drive a general—a man whose name I can no longer remember. I would pick up this fellow in the morning at his apartment and then would take him throughout the day wherever he had to go eventually bringing him back to his quarters. One morning I went to chauffeur him and arrived at his residence. His wife invited me in, as the general wasn't ready, and he wasn't going to be ready for a while. She handed me a can of brass polish and a rag. She said, "I want you to go out and polish the name plate on the door and the door knob and whatever other brass you see." I was stunned, and gave her a hard look. Slowly, I handed the polish and the rag back to her and adamantly refused. Looking her dead in the eye, I said, "Ma'am, with all due respect, I'm a soldier in the United States Army. I'm willing to die for my country, but I am *not* a servant and I am *not* polishing any doorknobs." I don't know whether or not that ever got reported back, but had it been I surely would have heard about it. I guess I was a bit arrogant, but I had too darn much pride to be a "dog robber" as they used to call it. That was when you were assigned to a general officer and you shined his shoes and acted like a valet. That was not for me.

GUARD DUTY

Even though I did chauffeuring duties, that didn't preclude my performing other types of duties in the army. One of the duties that I didn't much care for was guard duty, and I was assigned that fairly often. I don't recall exactly what the breakage was on it, but it was either two hours on and two hours off or two hours on and four off. However it was, it was for twenty-four hours at a time. We were each given a weapon and then were assigned to a post. We had to walk our posts. We were out there at two or three o'clock in the morning in the wintertime when the air was brittle cold and the stars were like diamonds with our feet crunching in the snow as we patrolled our posts. It was lonely, cold, and miserable and nothing was happening. Anybody with any brains was asleep. But we had to be so darn careful about being alert and ready for an incident that might occur.

I remember one time I went into the barracks to relieve myself and when I came out, the officer of the guard had caught up with me. He really chewed me out for not being on my post. I said, "No, sir, I was working my post but I needed to relieve myself, and I just stepped into the nearest barracks to do just that." I guess you weren't supposed to go to the john if you were on guard duty. I can see the merits of that, but this was not exactly a combat zone.

Another duty was guarding prisoners. We would get about twenty prisoners that we'd have to ride herd on, and some of these guys were hard timers. I mean, they were guys who were temporarily in the post guardhouse who were to be ultimately sent to federal prison for rape and murder and other serious capital crimes. These guys were losers. They would have taken off in a second, and we had to be so darn careful to keep our eyes on all these people. They were usually on work details until they were transferred to federal prisons, if that was where they were headed. Of course, a lot of them were guys who had goofed up and had a week or a couple of days in the guard house as company punishment. None of those guys did we have to worry about. But the hard cases always caused me a lot of concern, and I had my gun out of its holster a number of times. I never had to shoot one, though. As much as I hated the thought, it was his butt or mine, and I guarantee as long as I had the gun, it was going to be his butt.

Pfc. Richard Nabbe
A.S.N. 32920618
514ᵗʰ (H.M.) Ord. Co.
A.P.O. 230 c/o P.M. NYC, N.Y.

Pfc. Robert Nabbe
Motor Center Det.
South Post,
Fort Meyer,
Virginia

July 13, 1944

Dear Rob,

I haven't received a letter in about two months, but somehow one managed to seep through the other day and who should it be from, but you. Yep! It was written May 29 but believe me I truly enjoyed every bit of it.

Well Rob, this is the second birthday I have spent in the Army and I'm beginning to feel like I'm getting old. However, I should feel very happy because there are an awful lot over here that won't ever have a birthday again. The Co.C[35] did give me a birthday present though. Yep, he put me on guard to-nite. I don't suppose it was intentional so I bear no grudges.

I like France quite a lot better than England. It's an awful lot like back home. It's remarkable how much difference there can be in two countries so close together. Believe me, if I ever find that plug that keeps Great Briton afloat, I'll do those limeys a big favor and pull it out. There is actually more topsoil in our dust bowl back home than in all England itself. I swear I don't know how anything manages to grow on that rock.

When I first arrived in France we solely existed on rations, but now things are a lot better. Chow is a lot better than I ever expected to get, I'll tell you that. The countryside resembles a sieve more than anything else. The shells and bullets sure flew like hail for a while around here. Some of these towns are almost flat from shellfire. It beats me how the Frenchies lived through it.

Speaking of drinking, I haven't seen beer in months but, I did manage to get a load on once in France. When I first got here, me and a Buddy took off to a town near

---

35   Co.C. is a contraction for Company Commander, often an officer of low rank such as
     a 1st Lt.

by and bought a qt. of cognac and two qts. of wine. The whole price was about 1200 francs ($24.00) for the booze. Boy, was I ever drunk! While we were gone, our co. moved out and how I ever found them again is still a mystery. Believe me that cognac is wicked stuff. It goes down smooth, but after a bit, a guy nails you with a hammer and that's all you can remember. I woke up in somebody's back yard about four hours later. Don't ask me how I got there cause I don't know. After getting my bearings I found out I was going the wrong way from camp. Lucky I collapsed or I might be a prisoner of war or something by now. Oh me! What a life. Maybe I should have joined the W.T.C.U.[36]

I finally got assigned to an outfit and I like it a lot better. Believe me, the life of a casual is really hell. I don't won't any more of that for a long time.

Enclosed you will find a couple of pictures I filched from a Dutchman that got slightly ventilated. I don't think he will have any use for them anymore. I cut a few more odds and ends off his carcass before they patted him on the chest with a shovel but I can't send those through the mail. Notice how young these kids are in the German army. However, don't let looks deceive you. They know how to fight and they don't scare very easily either. I have a few more pictures I'll send you but they will come along later. Take good care of them cause they make good souvenirs.

Well kid that's all for now, so I'll bid thee adieu for a bit.

Thanks for the letter and I'll be seeing you soon. (I hope).

Your brother,
Rich

P.S. Give my regards to the old lady (Margie) and say hello to the kid.[37] That is, if its possible yet!

---

36   W.C.T.U. was a prohibition group—Women's Christian Temperance Union.

37   The "kid" Richard refers to in this letter is Robert and Marjorie's first child.

Pfc. Richard Nabbe
A.S.N. 32920618
514th (H.M.) Ord. Co.
A.P.O. 230 c/o P.M. N.Y.C.

Pfc. Robert Nabbe
Motor Center Detach.
2525th Service Unit
So. Post. Ft. Meyer
Virginia

Still lost in Normandy

August 1, 1944

Dear Robbie,

I say old chap, I have in the last few days, received about seventy letters. Among these, yours are very prevalent. I took about three hours out in the woods by myself and read all the mail I hadn't received for three months. Now my mail seems to be drifting in pretty well and I'm about up to date. Believe it or not, my most recent one is a letter from your own sweet little wife and a very nice one too. Of course, Mom runs a very close second. Irregardless, I had quite a bit of news to catch up on and I'm glad to know all goes well at home.

I'll tell you a little incident about my camera. I loaned it to a guy I knew who was working down the beach. And seeing how I couldn't get down there, I asked him to take a couple of shots for me. He did all right. My camera, him and his company moved out that day and so now I am "cameraless". Where he's at I don't know, but a Lt. in the company is going to locate it for me, and when I do, I'll fix that wise guy. Meanwhile, I borrowed a camera from a guy that takes my size film. I really appreciate your getting me all that film Rob and I'll surely repay you somehow. Boy, I missed some of the best shots you could ask for on account of that stinker. It seems you can't trust anybody anymore.

By the way old bean, I have been corresponding with Mildred[38] and she claims she is still that way about me. I'm wondering what to do about it! I still think the world of her, and I sincerely think she has changed for the better. Speaking of change, I've had lots of time to mull that courtship over in my mind and I came to the conclusion that I

---

38   Mildred is Mildred Veronica Mrzak, the woman Richard married after the war.

didn't do so good as being a beaux. In fact, I can see a few good points that would cause a girl to toss a certain person out on his ear. That is one thing this solitary confinement can do to you. Also I discovered that girls as nice and decent as she is, are very few and way far between. Comprè! So, I have decided to make a few amends and who can tell, maybe all will come out all right after all. Let's have your opinion eh?

I can realize that you don't get much time for yourself working all the time so I wouldn't blame you if you quit. Twenty four hours a day is more than one man can stand. Also, I imagine that job you have in the Army is just bubbling with monotony, so if you can get a transfer, snatch it up! I'll stick by you because I know how it is.

So R. Rice[39] has been in yonder parts here? Well, well! I wonder what cooks. I also hear Al. Lauer got hooked. I'm sorry I didn't get a line off to him, but of course I didn't know. Give him my congratulation if you see him.

Also, thanks for your birthday poem. I enjoyed it very much. I see you also have a touch of Shakespeare in you. Say, I'd love to go up to Rays[40] again. Just one night. Oh! Me! Here I am stranded. And what a place to be stranded in?

Old Betsy is running yet I see! Margie wrote and told me about all the work you did on her and also casually mentioned that all you needed was five new tires. My heart bleeds for you old boy. Well, maybe the rims will hold up for a time anyway.

I have grown me a mustache! Ye Gods, does it look like hell. I can't shave it off until I get home either. Me and my buddy have a bet on. So I guess I'll have to cultivate the seven little hairs into a pair of handle bars.

I hear about Herbies child arriving so I guess it's about time you started pounding the floor isn't it.[41] Wal, anyway let me know what develops.

If the next letter you get is written on toilet paper, you'll understand why! This is my last envelope and paper I have. Out here we can't buy anything because there ain't no place to buy it at. Logical deduction isn't it?

I'm afraid I'll have to leave you here for the time being so I'll thank you for all your letters you wrote to me and also for the film. If you can secure anymore, I'll surely appreciate it endlessly. Youze is a real pal. Bye for now and give my regards to everyone home. Once again, bye and thanks.

Your Brother
Rich

---

39 R. Rice is Robert Rice a friend from Monmouth, New Jersey.

40 Ray's was a nightspot where Robert and Marjorie went while they were dating.

41 Richard also refers to Robert's wife's impending delivery (which occurred on October 18, 1944).

Pfc. Richard Nabbe
A.S.N. 32920618
514th (H.M.) ORD. Co.
A.P.O. 230 c/o P.M. N.Y.C.

Pfc. Robert Nabbe
Motor Center Detach.
2525th Service Unit
So. Post, Ft Meyer
Virginia, U.S.A.

Still somewhere in France

August 7, 1944

Greetings "squire",

Your epistles have been arriving quite often to my delight. It seems all has been straightened out on this mail situation and I'm doing fine.

No Rob, as to day, I haven't received the films, but I'm sure they will come popping along any day now. I took a few pictures lately, but I can't say any of them are very good so far. Plenty of prospects, though.

Say, I'm certainly glad to hear you got a furlough. I know that job gets on your nerves so you can use it as far as I'm concerned. I don't know what the words mean.

You sure fixed old Betsey up too didn't you? You must have had a spurt of ambition to do all that work. It sounds like a good deal though and you and Marge will have lots of fun out of the old jalopy.

We are moving around quite a bit trying to keep up with the hienies[42] but I'm afraid they are advancing to the rear a little to fast for me. We got 'em going, old boy, and we ain't going to stop till we hit Berlin. I suppose we'll meet the Russians there but that's just fine as far as I'm concerned.

Last night I got a can on drinking some pretty potent alcohol and thought I was bronco bill, so I captured me a horse (we got a couple) and took off on him bare back. Wal now, its not as easy as it looks. I fell off, three times and to-day feel like a tank ran over me. Woe is me! I guess I'll leave it to the Indians to do that rough stuff.

Poor Dotty, she sure got all stung up didn't she! I remember once when I got stung

---

42 "heinies"—a pejorative for Germans.

by a bee in Califon, and I didn't laugh either! Remember?

Wal, it won't be long now old boy. I'll forward a pair of my hob nail shoes so you won't wear yours out pacing the floor![43] Don't worry Rob, we'll do it in shifts like guard duty. You walk an hour and I'll do the same! O.K.

Send any pictures you have along Rob. I love pictures. They make me feel like home again.

Enclosed is all the pictures I have left from that hienie. I'll give 'em to you sport. There is one negative too. Have it printed and let me know how it looks. That's all now.

Yer Brother

Rich

---

43 Pacing the floor refers to the eminent birth of Susan Carol Nabbe, Robert and
    Marjorie's first daughter, born on October 18, 1944.

WAR & NAVY
DEPARTMENTS
V-MAIL SERVICE
OFFICIAL BUSINESS

Pfc. Robert Nabbe
Motor Center Detach.
2525th Service Unit
So Post, Ft. Meyer, VA.

France

August 12, 1944

Dear Rob

I'd better try this for a change. It may get to you a lot faster. I have received your mail quite regularly now and I also got four rolls of film to-day. Nice going chum! I'm not working very hard now a days, in fact I sure could use some exercise. Just wait till we advance a little more and I may be sorry I made that statement. So your funds are low again tsk! You are simply extravagant. Now why aren't you like me? I got paid a week ago and I still have my pay (all except the twenty bucks I lost in a poker game). I guess you know why I have it? You guessed it! No place to spend any! I wish I could go swimming. I haven't swam in so long. I'm afraid I forgot how! If I ran into a bunch of babes undressed, I wouldn't leave, believe me. You don't have to, so thats that. I'll see ya chum —

Rich

WAR & NAVY
DEPARTMENTS
V-MAIL SERVICE
OFFICIAL BUSINESS

Pfc. Robert Nabbe
Motor Center Det.
2525 Service Unit
So. Post Ft. Meyer, VA

August 16, 1944

Dear Rob,

I can't see any sense in prosecuting those poor limays[44], so I guess you did the right thing. Ye gods, what I wouldn't do for a nice hunk of femininity right now! I am getting to a desperate point! Now and then, I manage to collar a quart of calvados, but that only results in a lovely hangover. Calvados, my friend, is our equivalent to two grains of cyanide! You can drink it like water, and is indeed very easy to take. And so, not considering its potent qualities, you continue to do so with no apparent ill effects. Then!! About a half hour later you are so plastered that you are completely reduced of all normal instincts and after a few back flips and a blood curdling scream fall flat on your puss! Nice country Rob, Lovely.

Adios,
Rich

---

44 Limays refers to Limeys, a slang term for British sailors.

Pfc. Richard Nabbe 32920618
514th (H.M.) Ord. Co.
A.P.O. 230 c/o P.M. N.Y.C.

Pfc. Robert Nabbe
Motor Center Detach.
2525th Service Unit
So. Post, Ft. Meyer VA.

August 21, 1944

Dear Rob,

As I lie here in my sanctuary of canvas, enduring a thin trickle of water which is saturating my person, I take my quill in hand, and out of sheer boredom, I emulate a heavy hearted privates tale of woe. By the way chum, not to interrupt that melodious strain of words above, that quill I referred to means "pen"! To continue: Out of the blissful sunny skies of Normandy, the huge billowing clouds of an August sky, departed and were surplanted by clouds of ominous dark and dreary blackness. The appearance of the landscape no longer remained colorful or breathtaking but were shrouded in a mist and the indescribable quietness of an impending storm. Then as though the bowels of heaven itself exploded, an avalanche of water descended to drench the ever parched land below. Now on this ever parched piece of land, whose exact location I cannot disclose, stood a small tent occupied by two liberators of the country they now occupy. So small and insignificant was this small adobe of canvas, that the endless sheets of water completely engulfed it and saturated its mournful occupants completely. From the interior of this canvas wall, a voice drifted. A voice so small and melodious, that it was barely audible above the shrieking deluge of water. But if one listens closely, he can detect a few words that are not destroyed by the fierceness of the gales fury. "I never saw such god-damned miserable weather in all my life" one light hearted carefree voice said. "These Frogs[45] can stick their weather up their fanny and their country with it," replied the other voice, with a merry twinkle resounding from his voice. "When the hell will this miserable ass aching war quit so we can go home" the first voice resounded.

"Ah! Quit yer bitchin and go to sleep in yer mud puddle will ya?" "Mud puddle is right, I knew if water ever hit these blankets it would be mud", replied the delightful answer. "Ya know, these blankets must be getting pretty dirty at that, we can't even

---

45   Frog is a pejorative for a Frenchman.

bend them any more unless they get wet". "Yeah and when they get wet we catch triple pneumonia, ah balls, ya can't win!" "Quit will ya, do you want to wake up my bull frog."

Act II

As we are waiting for the straight jackets to arrive, we tune in again on this unique conversation of these two happy soldiers of fortune (mis-fortune). Bill speaks "Say Dick[46], how would you like to have a woman here right now?"

D – "Jesus Christ, there you go again, if you don't stop chasing those sheep around in the next field we'll both get slapped in the chink."

B – "Aw, I wasn't gonna hurt 'em, I merely wanted to see if I could catch 'em!"

D - "Yeah! Well it's a damned good thing they can run faster than you, that's all I have to say". "You should be ashamed, and after going to church too"!

B – "Well I still think they are better looking than the women around here."

D – "What women?" "The only one I ever saw was about ten years old and her puss would scare the hienies all alone."

B.- "Pardner, you shore said a mouthful."

D - "We got any calvados left? I'm got a chill and could use a shot."

B - "No we ain't, and besides remember what happened the last time you took a shot." "It took three guys to carry ya back to the tent." "No more of that for us".

D – "Damn, this exciting life sure is hell, I figure in about two more weeks we'll be ripe for a section eight."

B – "Yup! When you start eating ivory soap for a laxative, I guess I purty near gone."

D - "You sure are a sad case all right."

Well, we'll leave these two happy souls all engrossed in their little paradise and turn ourselves once more to the weary path homeward. END.

You have just listened to another episode of our program entitled, "The Liberators Speak". Tune in again next week and again we'll interview these gallant, happy men of the Ord. Dept. Good bye all!

Well Rob, there you are! Silly? I suppose it is, but it's a letter. You may enjoy a small part of our existence over here. Lets hope its not like we do!

So long kid and keep struggling -

Your Bud,
Richie

---

46   Dick is probably Richard as many of his friends called him Dick.

Pfc. Richard Nabbe 32920618
514th (H.M.) Ord. Co.
A.P.O. 230 c/o P.M. N.Y.C.

Pfc. Robert Nabbe
Motor Center Detach.
2525th Service Unit
So. Post, Ft. Meyer, VA.

August 26, 1944

Dear Rob,

Been on the move, so I had to wait till your mail caught up to me before I could answer.

I write to all you folks as often as I can, but when we are on the move I can't quite keep up with it. I do manage to keep pretty well up to date with Mom though. You sure said a mouthful when you said Mom was a great person. I don't think any one can replace or surpass anything she has been or will be. Thanks for letting me know her birthday is due. I'd never know if you hadn't reminded me. In answer to your questions, I'll do the best I can under the circumstances. We aren't permanently established, we are a complete mobile outfit. We move up as the infantry does or whenever we are needed. In simple words I'll answer your questions as follows, one, no, two, yes, three, yes, four, yes, five, no, six, yes.[47] In this way I won't divulge any military information so it should be OK.

Yes I did receive four rolls of film, but the others didn't as yet arrive. It should be here soon though as it's been a time since I received the last four. The wrapping was a master piece but my ingenuity got it open all right.

Your picture is gratefully received Rob, and I think it looks a lot like you. Many thanks chum! That was a swell idea you had about the picture folder. I'd sure have liked

---

47 Enclosed in the letter is a small document written by Robert. It contained a list of names and phone numbers (each one had only five digits), but also the questions Richard answered in this paragraph.

  Question 1: Are you stationed in one spot?
  Question 2: Are you moving up behind the inf. (infantry)?
  Question 3: Are you near the fighting?
  Question 4: Are you behind the lines?
  Question 5: Are you engaged in actual combat?
  Question 6: Are you doing ord (ordnance) work behind the lines?

that I know. However, if it didn't turn out so good, it's all right, it's not your fault. You know, we take a lot of pride in our pictures, it's one way we have of holding a conversation with the French. We just pull out our pictures and continue to bore the hell out of them, but we feel better. Say Rob, I wonder if you could dig up a wallet or picture holder with a lot of windows in it. My wallet is falling apart and I sure could use a new one. Seeing as how I haven't much money, I need it for the pictures much more. I sent home to ma for some paper and envelopes, so don't bother sending any Rob. It will save you a bit of trouble anyhow.

I'm glad to hear that Ruth and Herbie and child are coming home, I'd sure like to see the family again. Let me know if they make it home and how it all came out. Have a little fun son. Also old top, pretty soon comes the floor pacing. Just remember, I'm right with you, so when you labors begin (not Margies) I'll be with you in spirit.

Thanks a load for the advice you so kindly analyzed.[48] Your philosophy is pretty sound and it coincides with my own very much. I received another letter from Mickey and she seems to feel quite the same as before, and as I said before, she seems to have become a great deal matured and my attitudes and views have gone to a different view since I have been in the Army, so I'll see what results when I get home. Maybe when she sees what a wreck I am she will change her mind. In the meantime we are corresponding and all seems to go very well.

We have great hopes that the war will be over soon here. We are doing fine, and I guess by now you knew that Paris fell to the Allies. One more for us. No, I don't think it will be long now.

I thought that Mrs. Tobin[49] was extremely kind indeed to send me those papers, and that letter I wrote her was merely a small way that I thought I could repay her. However, I am by no means the saint you picture me to be. I'll admit I do go to church on Sunday (I feel funny as hell too!) and enjoy it too. Maybe I have changed a bit, but I'm sure I don't notice it.

Ye gods Rob, why the hell don't you scrap that trap of yours?[50] I never knew anyone could have so much trouble with one heap of tin as you do. Maybe I can ship you a jeep. Lord knows we have plenty over here. I haven't seen any other vehicles than G.I. for a

---

48   Richard previously asked his brother, Robert, for advice about resuming his relationship with Mildred Mrzak, his former girlfriend. Robert was against it and advised Richard to take things slowly. Here Richard calls Mildred by her nickname, "Mickey."

49   Mrs. Tobin is Robert's mother-in-law, Jessie Isabel Holmes Tobin.

50   Richard suggests that Robert dump his old car, but cars were difficult to obtain during World War II, so many people kept patching and fixing up what they had as best they could.

long time now. I'm beginning to believe there aren't any other kind. It's now so damned dark I can't see anymore. However, I'll continue by feel method.

I'm sure Margie is fine and outside of you calling her "pumpkin belly" she is in her glory. I'm equally glad to hear Mom is so good too!

Well Rob, say hello to the Hertleins if you see them for me and don't drink my liquor too fast. Thanks for the lengthy epistles and enclosed you will find a couple of stamps from Germany. Guess whose ugly puss is on them?[51]

As you say, Bone Server[52]
Your Bud, Richie

---

51   The stamps are German stamps with Hitler's face on them.
52   Richard phonetically spells the French phrase bonsoir (good night) as Bone Server.

KITCHEN POLICE

Another one of the mundane duties was K.P. If you weren't a corporal or a sergeant, if you were a Private First Class—which I still was at that point—or a private, you did kitchen duty and that was a lo-o-o-ng day. I think the barracks orderly came in at about five in the morning and shined a flashlight in your face to wake you up to get dressed and to report to the kitchen where you would spend a long day taking orders and performing menial tasks like peeling mountains of potatoes or washing hundreds of dishes.

At Fort Myer, there was a limited amount of mess facility and a maximum amount of men. I guess in peacetime it was a well-balanced military installation, but in wartime, it was overcrowded. Rather than mess kits or compartmented trays, the tables were set family style with the food placed in bowls and platters and everyone helped himself to whatever he wanted. Ultimately though, that did get changed over to our using mess trays, which was a lot less complicated.

Fort Myer was originally an officer's training post so things were set up a little bit differently there than it would have been for enlisted men. The eating off of plates and drinking out of cups was a hangover from when the officers were being trained there. We fed two hundred men per mess, and we did three messes a meal. That was six hundred people, three times a day and involved cleaning up two hundred dishes, two hundred cups, two hundred forks, two hundred knives, two hundred plates, two hundred bowls, two hundred whatever. Our job was getting all this washed and then resetting the table for the next group of people.

The mess sergeant would blow the whistle, and here would come this thundering herd of guys scrambling to eat. After a sitting, the guys on K.P. duty cleared the tables, swept the floors, washed the table tops, washed all the dishes, and reset the tables. This was done three times each meal, and by the time the work was finished, it was somewhere around eleven o'clock at night. This went on seven days a week for as long as you were assigned that duty. You could figure on having K.P. duty for seven days at least. It literally tore you up daily because after you finished the dishes after the last mess, you had all the pots and pans to wash, and they really were the tough part of it. Then you also peeled potatoes, the old army standard of peeling potatoes, which you would peel by the bushels every day.

ARMY FOOD

We used to get a lot of what I called goats, which was actually sheep or mutton. I think we shipped all our beef to Australia, and the Australians shipped all their sheep to us because we never saw beef. We saw mutton, and I couldn't stand to smell it cooking. To this day, I can't stand the smell of mutton cooking or lamb. The smell nauseates me because when I was in the army I stood for days and days smelling that stuff as it cooked. It was prepared in many ways. We'd have lamb stew and we'd have roast lamb, and I guess lamb burgers—any way the cooks could figure to cook that carcass. It got to the point where I couldn't eat it, and I still can't. We also used to get a lot of by-products, like beef hearts and liver that similarly turned me off forever after. Two army foods I continue to like to this day, however, are Spam and chipped beef on toast. It wasn't the kind of food that I was raised on, though. For the most part army guys ate everything in sight! Most weren't chauffeurs—only a few of us were—and those that weren't worked in heavy duty capacities resulting in their having eager appetites.

At the end of a K.P. day, you had to clean up the grease traps. That was an awful job. It was nauseating. Then there were all of the garbage cans that had to be scrubbed down with hot soapy water, rinsed and thoroughly sanitized. It was really for the well-being of everybody. You don't need any diseases originating from unclean containers and cooking vessels. When we got finished—they used to call it pearl diving—our hands would come out of that water super clean. We used really hot water and when our hands came out of it they were shrunken up like claws and bleached out. Talk about clean fingernails! I never had such clean fingernails in my life.

PERKS OF K.P.

One of the good sides of being on K.P. was that when the others had powdered eggs for breakfast a person on K.P. got fresh fried eggs instead. (There was always a small supply of eggs for cooking purposes.) In addition, the cook would fix you anything you wanted. Back in those days, I'd have a half a dozen fried eggs and a pile of potatoes. I ate like a king. If the cook liked you—if you worked hard—the cook responded to your efforts. His job was easier if you worked harder. I had one in particular who would say, "Work hard, and I'll bake you a pie." I dearly love pineapple pie with crumbs on it. He'd make me pineapple pie with crumbs and I'd sit and eat the whole thing in one sitting. It was something! This was one of the most pleasant memories from my army days that has stayed with me all these years later.

INTELLIGENCE FILES

There were times when I'd be driving a general to a distant army post for one reason or another. I recall a number of them. I remember going one time to Camp Ritchie, Maryland. Later on after World War II I believe President Eisenhower used Camp Ritchie as a retreat, but back in the days during the war it was a military intelligence center. One time I transported a general to Camp Ritchie, and I was put in a room to wait for him while he conducted this business. It was a huge room with all these file drawers around it. Every wall had little filing-card sized file drawers like old library card catalogues. There were hundreds of these files. One of the commissioned officers was in the room, and I asked him, "What's the purpose of all this?" And he said, "You can go look, if you'd like." I opened a drawer and inside was a picture and a file on every German soldier that our intelligence was aware of. Also included was a history of the guy's existence. If he were dead, the card would say, "killed" or "missing in action". I thought to myself, "Holy smoke, the Germans must have the same thing on us because their intelligence is excellent."

Pfc. Richard Nabbe
32920618
514th (H.M.)[53] Ord. Co.
A.P.O. 230 % P.M. N.Y.C.

Pfc. Robert Nabbe
M.C.D. 2525 Service Unit
So. Post, Ft Meyer VA.

September 9, 1944

Dear Rob,

*I received two letters from you to-day and also the photographs too. Thanks a lot for
the pictures Rob. I like them immensely and they certainly do bring back memories to
me. You got a couple of dandy shots of the river and I am certainly going to hold on to
them for old times sake. That one picture of Margie is a pip. However I think you are
the one who should read that book and not her. I also received some pictures from Dot
that I took in Camp Reynolds and they came out fine. From looking over them, I can
realize just what a crummy place it was. I'd much rather be out in the fields in a pup
tent any day, than be stuck back in that hole. In fact, I can truthfully say that the best
times I ever had in the army is right here in France. You may live a little rougher but you
don't have all that chicken shit to contend with. You do your work and that's all there is
to it. Our officers leave us alone and everyone gets along just dandy!*

*I don't know how much Gabriel Heater[54] says about the war but I'll give you
my version and you can deduct your own conclusions. So far today, I saw thirty—nine
truck loads of prisoners go by and that goes on that way every day. We are going like
hell to keep up with our combat units and the Germans are retreating so fast that we
have all we can do to keep up with them. Believe me Rob, it won't be long when we'll
be in Germany. All I see is wrecked German tanks and equipment. I swear I don't
know how they hold out. In short words, we are kicking the hell out of them. I got the
swastika off a German plane that was shot down near us. It was on the tail, so I got
a cold chisel and a hammer and whacked it off. I also whacked a lot of hide off of me,
but I licked the blighter. I don't know how I'll be able to get it home cause its so big, but*

---

53   In Richard's return address, (H.M.) means "Heavy Maintenance".

54   Gabriel Heatter was an American radio commentator whose World War II era sign-
     on—"There's good news tonight"—became his catchphrase.

I'll try. I never saw so many bullet holes in one plane as this one had. It was actually a flying sieve. I'll need a truck to carry all my souvenirs in pretty soon if this don't quit.

I spoke to our captain about my camera and he is personally going to write a letter to the company commander of the guy who has my camera. Maybe I'll get some results from that. I hope so anyway.

So Herbie and family got home all right eh? I'm glad to hear it. I'll bet they were glad to get home once again. Speaking of babies, how is yours coming? I imagine Jr. should be on the way pretty soon. I can see your sweating it out right now. My sympathies old bean.

Well Rob, I must go now so I'll close this uninteresting masterpiece. Keep old Bessie running and give my love to the little woman. So

"Au plaisir de vous revoir!![55]

Your Bud
Richie

That phrase means (Goodbye till we meet again)

---

55 Richard had a facility for learning languages and quickly became quite adept at speaking French phonetically, though at times, his phonetic spellings of French were amusing.

Pfc. Richard Nabbe – 32920618
514th (HM.) Ord. Co.
A.P.O. 230, c/o P.M., N.Y.C.

Sept 14, 1944

Dear Rob,

This was written a couple days ago, but I have had a miserable head cold and I haven't been worth a damn. However, I now summon all my energy and will get it to you somehow. This poem was meant to be on your birthday.

"To Youze on Yer Birthday"

I know it's only once a year,
To you, I send this poem of cheer.
But still I know no other way
In which to celebrate this day.
At twenty-five you're quite a guy,
And a lot of years have sure gone by.
Yup! Lots of years, and how they flew
With Mom and Dad and Dot and you.
But now your life has just begun
And up ahead there's lots of fun
You have a wife and baby too!
And that's a joy that's just for you!
I know right now it's stormy weather,
But someday we may be together
To have the fun that we once had,
With smiles and joy and not be sad.
I know you lead a life of sin,
Just raising hell and drinking gin.
Now don't get mad and don't get sore,
Just stick around, there's plenty more.
Now pretty soon you'll be a pop,
And more than once you'll blow your top.
Because the floor you'll have to walk

And listen to old Jr. squawk.
Now if you have a little son,
I'm sure the beer will start to run,
But if you have a little daughter,
The Potomac with lose some river water
(And you know what I mean too!!)
Alas an uncle I shall be
No matter whether he or she,
So I had better hurry back
So the kid can bounce me on his lap (optimistic)
A birthday poem, this was meant to be,
But strangely enough as you can see,
The subject has kind of gone astray
And I forgot what I started to say.
Well Rob, just try and think of me,
Away across the god-damned sea,
Just wishin' I was there with you,
A drinkin' booze till I turned blue
But we can't do that cause I'm still here,
So the next time you go drink some beer,
Instead of one, you just drink two,
And make believe that I'm with you.
No matter how far away I dwell,
Your brother thinks your still damned swell.
He also hopes, if hopes come true.
That the next twenty-five, he'll spend with you.

___________*Finis*_________

Happy Birthday Rob and I hope your day will be pleasant. If Shakespeare ever heard this, he's blown his brains out with a cross bow!

Recently, I received a couple letters from you and I see that you still maintain a very wicked life. Some of these days I'll get a letter edged in black and find that you got buried with your jeep as a coffin. Easy does it chum! I just got a shot too, and for once my arm doesn't hurt. I'm getting immune I guess! I got a cold instead. I prefer the sore arm myself. You tell those diplomats to shag ass back here cause we need cannon fodder. Believe me chum, it can't last much longer now. So you want to know what Calvados is eh? Well, I'll try to describe it to you! Well it's about twice as strong as our whiskey and it would burn the ass hole out of ________________ (indecipherable) man. It's so potent that half of a shot evaporates before it hits your mouth. After a few hookers you don't feel drinks so you decide that it's lousy stuff and try to drink it like water. Now that's your mistake! You are perfectly sober for about a half-hour and then all of a sudden you are so god-damned plastered you can't even see. Then in about ten minutes the climax comes and you are out cold. And I mean cold!! I learned my lesson and I leave it alone now. Yes, it sure is powerful stuff. I'll take some nitric acid if it's all the same to you.

Well kid I'll say so-long so I can recuperate.

Be good, stay drunk and
I'll be seeing ya!

Your brother
Richie

Pfc. Richard Nabbe – 32920618
514th (H.M.) Ord. Co.
A.P.O. 230 c/o P.M. N.Y.C.

Pfc. Robert Nabbe
Motor Center Detach.
2525th Service Unit
South Post Ft. Meyer
VA.

Belgium (rain)

October 4, 1944

Dear Rob,

I know I haven't been writing too often but I can't chase Hienies and write too! That's not sarcasm Rob, it's the truth! The weather is a lot colder than I would like it to be and I'm slowly freezing. I have a sneaking suspicion I'll be here for the winter and God only knows how long I'll last then. Also, we move so damned often it's a shame. You know what I mean, one or two days here and then pull stakes. The change of scenery is dandy, but my constitution is against it. I suspect I'll wind up in Germany in a day or two. It's amazing how the attitude of the people changes as we get nearer Germany. They just stare at you as though you were poison. Now is when we have to be careful. G.I. Joes are found missing or shot or something every day and it isn't AWOL either. The nearest I want to come to any Germans, soldiers or civilians is rifle range. They are a tricky lot all right and it only takes one slip to make you brotherless. American soldiers trust anyone and that's bad. I suppose we'll lose a couple out of the company before they wise up. We were out at a artillery company for a couple days to service their guns. We were parked about fifty feet from their 155 long toms[56], and no kidding Rob, every time they let loose they blow you a foot off the ground. Christ, they would scare any body to death. We pulled the black out shades down in the truck, when they let loose and blew the shade rollers and all right out of the frames with the concussion. That night the Siegfried line[57] really caught hell because I just bounced like a ball in my back sack all night. Result, no sleep! Those guys claim you get used to it,

---

56   155 long tom is a heavy artillery piece.
57   The Siegfried line was a strategic defensive line on the German border.

but I'll be damned if I can see it. I'd be a total nervous wreck in a week. Phooey on the artillery.

I did manage to get a couple hours in when we passed through Paris. No kidding Rob, it's a paradise of paradises. I never saw such lovely women or such a nice place in all my life. Paris is all they say and more. If I ever get a chance to go back, you can bet your life I will. It's very similar to Washington, only better. That's the best I can do as far as description goes. Enclosed you will find one of our safe conduct passes. Our planes drop them by the hundreds of thousands and they cover the ground like snow in places. Another piece of junk for you.

I received three letters from you and that's all the mail I received in a week. Say Rob, if you have some spare cigarettes lying around send some to your brother will you please. The cigarettes subject is critical here and we don't know when we will get smokes again. It may sound funny to you, but that's the way it is.

I admire your optimism about the war old boy, but the way things are going, it looks like its going to stretch out a bit. At any rate I sincerely hope you are right. That Siegfried line is one tough baby, but we'll crack it and damned soon too.

Say I'm sorry about that boy who got killed Rob. I know how you must feel. It's a tough situation and I'm sure that something will develop soon. We have our troubles with the same situation as you have, but we solve ours a lot easier. (a nickel bullet!) comprē.

I'm glad you had a nice birthday old bean. Maybe next year I'll be there to help celebrate it with you. Say how about J.H. getting married? That's a surprise all right! Poor guy. I guess he has gone berserk!!

Well Rob, don't be surprised if one of these fine days you hear from me where Joe is, or at least somewhere there abouts. We keep getting latrine —o —grams on that subject quite regularly and just between you and me, I don't like it a damned bit. Oh what a future I've got ahead of me. Sometimes I wonder?

Well Old Chap, that about all for now so I'll say so long for now. Thanks for your swell letter Rob.

Bye Now
Yer Brudder
Richie

PS I sweated out that dose I thought I got in Brussels and so far I'm` Ok. Whew! Let hope I don't catch any VDs. I sure wouldn't want that.

Pfc. Richard Nabbe
A.S.N. 32920618
514ᵗʰ Ord (HM) Co.
A.P.O. 230
c/o P.M N Y. C.

Pfc. Robert Nabbe
Motor Center Detach.
2525 Service Unit
So. Post, Ft. Meyer, VA.

Somewhere in Belgium

Oct 11, 1944

Dear Rob,

Sorry about the delay old bean, but I am having trouble with my mail writing here. I suppose Margie has had her baby by now, so lets hear from you soon. I want all the details if I can possible get them.

It has been fairly decent here of late, as far as weather is concerned. We have quite a lot of rain, but it doesn't get real cold like it did a while back. You know, it seems funny, where you mention summer uniforms because I have worn O.Ds[58] for so long now that I have forgotten what summer khaki is like. All I do remember is that they are awfully hard to keep clean. You have my deepest sympathy.

---

58 O.Ds refer to "olive drab" uniforms. Robert explains: "O.D.'s refer to winter G.I. uniforms meaning heavy woolen clothes dyed olive drab for less conspicuous notice by the enemy. Now it is all 'camouflage'. Summer uniforms were cotton—also called 'chino'—tan colored (not dark) and typically called "sun tans". They were a pain to keep clean, and as a chauffeur I was outfitted with '3 Class A' suntan uniforms in order to always look neat for my higher-level function driving generals. You were always told when to change uniforms each season as it approached from Sun Tans to O.D.s and back. Since I was permanently based, for a fee I could have my sun tans laundered at the Post laundry (gov't run). If I was broke I'd launder them myself on a plank—a G.I. brush (floor type) and Octogon yellow laundry soap. After they dried I would press them carefully. There were ironing boards in the laundry room of the barracks and Aunt Carrie gave me a used iron [that] I kept under lock and key or it would have quickly been stolen." [Aunt Carrie was Carrie Koelsch Smith, older sister of Robert and Richard's mother, Edna Mae Koelsch Nabbe.]

Say Rob, that hurricane must have raised particular hell back home. It did a lot of damage to the old homestead. How do we rate such things anyway? Poor old Jersey catches all the hell, and such a little state too!

By now I guess the canvas has worn through on your rubberless tires. Well Rob you have a couple thousand miles left on the rims yet. You should see the tons of tires we had stacked up that had been shot to hell. Brand new tires full of bullet holes and shrapnel. I'll just have to sympathize with youse old boy.

By the looks of things, I'm going to be here all winter, and believe me Rob, I don't like that at all. Our winter issue of clothes just came through which doesn't indicate anything but disaster. Send me a pair of snow shoes pronto and a dog sled.

Thanks for sending me the folders I asked for. If you like, you can send it any way you please. I have received no packages to late and I suppose I'll have to wait a bit for their arrival because mail comes real slow these days. Boy, I'll really get a bunch when I do though. All I hope is that you wrapped them pretty strong because if you didn't, they won't be worth a dime. You would be surprised at the amount of packages that we throw away because they are so beat up that the contents can't be recognized.

At present I'm doing guard duty all the time and nothing happens of interest to write about. In other words, I'm stuck!!

Well Robbie, that will have to do for now, so I'll write again real soon. I hope the baby turns out all right old chap. Be good and try not to kill yourself running around in Washington.

Yer bruther
Richie

Pfc. Richard Nabbe – 32920618
514ᵗʰ (H.M.) Ord. Co.
A.P.O. 230
c/o P.M. N.Y.C. N.Y.

Pfc. Robert Nabbe
Motor Center Detach.
2525ᵗʰ Service Unit
So. Post, Ft. Meyer VA.

"A la Belgique"

October 17, 1944

Dear Rob,

I completely understand your circumstances about the baby, and I can certainly realize how you feel.[59] I don't expect to hear from you so very often, as long as I get a line from you once in a while. I'm more than satisfied. I can't write to you as much as I would like to, but I do my best and I'm afraid it will have to do. Well I surmise by now, Jr. has arrived and you can resort to a more peaceful existence once more. I think I ask about Margie in every letter I have written for the past two months. I hope to receive news of the happy event soon.

Rob, if dreams come true, I sure hope the ones you have come true. I can't even dream of home any more, so you can see what hopes I have here. Well when I do arrive home, we'll really tie on a snootful that will last a month. In the mean time you old SOB[60], you better ease off the booze or you will embalm yourself. I shouldn't speak to loud, because I sure got plenty drunk over here quite a few times. In Belgium (here) you can buy beer that is pretty good and with a quart of cognac, it's even better than that. These civilians don't know what a boiler maker is and they stand behind you so that they can catch you as you fall. Of course they underestimate American constitutions and stand with their jaw dropping as we knock one after another off. You understand that eventually you do fall down, but it takes one hell of a lot to do it.

Please don't talk about G.I. culinary art to me. I know exactly what it's like. You would really appreciate what I mean if you were here. For instance: If our cooks ever

---

59   Susan was born the day after this letter was written.
60   SOB is an acronym for son of a bitch.

lost their can opener, we would starve to death in two days. That's a fact. No kidding I have a letter "K" growing on my chest.[61] That's how many I have eaten since I have been over here. OH! I'll never eat another cracker as long as I live!! Solemn oath!!

You don't have to tell me anything about Dot. I took her out myself and I know what a swell kid she is. In fact I would rather take her out than most girls. I have more fun. My sympathies are extended. I'll send you a camouflaged suit so you can duck Mrs. Lauer[62] when she comes down the street. My how that female can talk! Alby got a quick ride, didn't he? I at least had a little while at home, but he didn't get much to speak of. Who knows, maybe they need more overseas?

I picked up a German Luger over here and it sure is nice. I test fired it and it hasn't hardly any kick at all. Those Germans sure do put out nice equipment. Well they had plenty of time to make it, so I guess it should be good.

You guessed right Rob, it is kind of cold over here and about January it gets about 15 degrees below zero. Ain't we gonna have fun? Our job isn't to stay in one spot, Rob, we move whenever we are needed. As soon as the Siegfried Line is cracked, we'll be off again I suppose. Only this time it will be Germany and not Belgium. At present I'm not being shot at. The reason for that is because I shoot first and don't give them the chance. You remember on guard how you shout "halt" three times and then shoot? Well we shoot first and then say halt! Not a good policy, but you'd be surprised how much healthier one stays that way. That's all for now Rob, so I'll sign off for now with "keep sober."[63]

---

61 Richard says, "I have a letter 'K' growing on my chest." Here he is referring to the K-ration, an individual daily combat food ration, originally intended as an individually packaged daily ration for issue to airborne troops, tank corps, and other mobile forces for short durations. The K ration provided three meals per day—breakfast, lunch, and dinner. A major criticism of the K-ration was its inadequate caloric and vitamin content to meet the needs of soldiers in battle because ration planners did not realize the enhanced caloric needs of soldiers who were fighting in extreme conditions.

62 Mrs. Lauer was a neighbor in Irvington and Albert's (Alby's) mother. Robert states, "She was the gabbiest person in the city of Irvington."

63 By this time Richard was in the thick of the fighting. He served both in the D-Day Invasion and the Battle of the Bulge. During one night battle, he was running across the battlefield and tripped over a piece of an engine. It tore a hole in the side of his lower leg that was still not completely healed forty-five years later! At one point doctors wanted to amputate Richard's leg in his later years, but he refused. Eventually, the wound completely healed—not long before Richard died—but there was a large dent in his leg with skin stretched only over the bone. In later years Robert said that Richard went to war as a happy-go-lucky kid and came back a changed man, sober and a bit sour on life. He refused to discuss the war and the only thing he would tell his brother was this: "When your country dehumanizes you to the point where you

Your bruther,
Richie

Washington, D.C.,
17 January 1946

Received on this date from Major W. D. Kelly, QMC, War Department Motor

Center, The Pentagon, Washington, D.C., the sum of Twenty Dollars ($20.00)

for use in connection with an official trip to Camp Ritchie, Maryland, and

Carlisle, Pennsylvania.

_______________________________ 32578454
(Name and ASNo)

T/5 MCD WDMP
____
(Rank and Organization)

RECEIPT FOR $20. FOR TRIP TO CAMP
RITCHIE, MARYLAND

can use dead bodies as furniture to sit on while you eat your meals, what have you become?"

PRISONERS OF WAR

I remember also being up in Baltimore where they had a lot of German prisoners of war. Those guys were still arrogant even though they were prisoners of war and were in this country. A lot of them stayed on after the war or at least came back. They liked the United States much better than Germany and I can understand why.

I also remember Italian prisoners who were brought to this country. In the ethnic Italian-American neighborhood they would seal off the street and have a block dance and refreshments for the Italian prisoners. Those Italian soldiers were mostly harmless and low risk prisoners. They didn't want to fight for the Axis anyhow. They would rather have fun. Guarding them was easy.

WEAPONS TESTING

At Camp Ritchie they were testing the effects of our anti-tank weapons on captured German tanks and other military equipment that had been brought over from the battlefields. While I was there I was able to observe the tests along with the general I was chauffeuring. They towed these tanks across the field and then would fire our anti-tank devices at them. For the most part, the stuff would just bounce off. German tanks—those Tiger tanks—were formidable. They were very, very difficult to stop, and I was a witness as to why.

A SPECIAL MEAL

I hadn't eaten in the course of that day and I mentioned this to the general officer. I said, "I don't know what arrangements have been made for me to have something to eat." He took me down to the officer's mess. There was a master sergeant there and the general officer said, "Fix this man a meal and give him anything he wants." Of course, you never argue with a general! The sergeant didn't take too kindly to a lousy PFC being treated like, you know, an officer. He grudgingly asked, "What would you like?" And I said, "Well, the general said I could have anything I want. I'd like a steak and mushrooms." I got it, too. I will not forget that. It was quite a treat to me after having had so much lamb. Having a real piece of meat was a delicacy. That meal was so memorable I vividly recall it today.

WEAPONS TESTING ON ANIMALS

Another time, I went to Camp A. P. Hill in Virginia with a general. We were observing exercises that were pretty cruel to animals. They were testing devices for getting Japanese soldiers out of caves in the Pacific Theater when they wouldn't surrender. Different methods were being tested that might force the Japanese either to come out or to be killed inside the cave. Instead of having live prisoners to test, they used goats, sheep, and hogs. They put the animals in the caves and then used different incendiary devices and different explosives to see if they would die. After the smoke cleared away, whatever was left alive would come running out and the soldiers would shoot them. Then their lungs and other organs were analyzed to see whether or not there were toxins that would help kill enemy soldiers.

War is hell—hardly an exercise in civility. Any way one could dispose of the enemy, I guess was considered fair game and this was one of the means they tried.

A CLOSE CALL

What I do recall best about being at Camp A.P. Hill was driving down a road that troops accompanied by some tanks had just marched through. It was all dusty and you could hardly see. The general told me to return to where we had originated. I turned around and was coming back, and I almost got crushed by an army tank. The tank driver didn't see me and I didn't see him. It was at the last minute that both of us managed to avoid each other. That was a pretty close call.

Pfc. Richard Nabbe
A.S.N. 32920618
514th Ord (HM) Co.
A.P.O. 230
c/o P.M. N.Y.C. N.Y.

Pfc. Robert Nabbe
Motor Center Detach.
2525th Service Unit
So. Post, Ft. Meyer, VA.

"Belgium" yet

November 4, 1944

Dear Robbie,

*Alas, I can see your locks turning white as your aching dogs prance from one end
of the barracks to the other. You are going through what is commonly known as "Papa-
itis". (Yer bruther ain't doing bad either.)*

*Say why don't you do like the farmers do and reach in and snatch the kid by the foot
and drag him out.[64] Or maybe they aren't doing that this year? Well cheer up Rob, he's
got to let go sometime, he's just got the stubborn Nabbe streak, but you can warm his ass
for him later on for it.*

*Cheer up chum and let me tell you how nice and cozy it is over here. We are billeted
in an old barn and it has no heat. It's a fire trap that's why. We sleep on the bare floor
and you spend most of the night just turning over to keep the shades of blue nice and
even. Fun, eh? Well it's only the beginning chum. It's quite chilly right now, but the worst
hasn't started yet. From all indication I'll sweat the Winter here and I'm not happy at
all. So! The next time your friend opens the door of the fire you are toasting in, just tell
him you have a brother who would sure like to be sitting next to you. We were issued
over coats recently, but it's not because they wanted to it's because it took too much
gasoline in our blow torches to thaw the boys out so they could work.*

*The Hienies are up to their old tricks again. They sneak around in a plane and
drop great big colored eggs on us when we aren't looking. Yesterday I saw one go off, but
lucky me just wasn't close enough to get an honorable discharge. Of course a change of*

----

64   Richard, unaware that the baby had been born, assumed that Susan would be a boy.

underwear was necessary, but that just keeps you from getting constipated. I was near a couple of M.P.'s when this young tornado let go and it did my heart good to see his face turn a sickly white and his nice stripped [sic] helmet dance on the tip of his curly locks. I wonder what I looked like. Well it blew a great big hole in the ground, plus a couple houses, plus its civilian contents, so it didn't do much damage at that. That was only the third time in one day we had a visit from our (censored) friends. Yer bruther is on the verge of a total nervous collapse. I eat with a rubber fork and drink my coffee from a paper cup so I don't knock out my teeth and stab hell out of myself. Yes, "LIFE IS ROUGH IN THE E.T.O!!

I'm glad you like my poetic birthday contribution. It's a pretty cheap present, but at least you know I ain't fertilizer so that's something.

I'm glad J.H.'s[65] wedding turned out all right. I wish I could have been there myself.

Well Rob, I guess this will have to suffice for now so I'll say so long. Take it easy or you'll be a nervous wreck like me pretty soon. Of course you'll have a better time getting yours, but the symptoms are the same.

Yer luvin bruther
Richie

---

65   J.H. is Jimmy Horahan, a family friend.

Pfc. Richard Nabbe – 32920618
514ᵗʰ (H.M.) Ord. Co.
A.P.O. 230
c/o P.M. N.Y.C.

Pfc. Robert Nabbe
Motor Center Detach.
2525ᵗʰ Service Unit
So. Post, Ft Meyer,
Virginia

Belgium

November 11, 1944

Dear Rob,

Well chum, at last the great event has taken place. Let me offer my humble congratulations to you and Margie. You can start right now to get new soles for your shoes and once again assume the role of a safe human being. I feel a lot better about the whole thing myself now that it's all over. Where did you find the name of "Susan"? It sure is a swell one and I can truthfully say your choice is excellent. Now I have a niece named "Suzie." I hope I get home in time to see her graduate from high school.[66]

I received a letter from the Hertliens and it was about three months old. It was a swell letter though and it was sure nice to hear from them once more. They were having trouble with their so called "urchin" but I hope by now it has passed over all that and is finally on its way to growing up.

At present, the weather is decidedly bad. It is awfully muddy and its either rained or snowed for the last week. It's cold and miserable, but we aren't so bad off as the boys up front. I was in Germany a couple days ago, and talk about a mess. A guy digs a slit trench and in an hour it's a bath tub. There's more mud up there than there is trees and its all woods. Knee deep is the average depth. I got a cold and so has most of the country I guess. How in the hell do they expect us to win a war if it rains and snows all the time. So help me I'll "moider"[67] the weather man.

Mail is exceptionally slow right now, but I suppose when it does arrive, it will come

---

66 Richard did live to see Susan graduate from high school in June 1962.
67 "Moider" translates to murder.

in a big bunch. Where we are staying, its so cold at night my fingers freeze and I can't write. We are really out of civilization right now. We are in the woods and plenty of mountains to boot. Its lovely scenery, but I won't vouch for its comfort as far as a soldier goes. This letter seems to have turned into a bitch session, but I got to tell somebody you know chum. After you live this gypsy life for about six months and with no relief in sight as far as going home is concerned, you start getting section eight ideas.[68] Excuse me this time chum, maybe I can make the next letter more cheerful.

So now you work as a coalman? Well Rob I'll grant you this much, you got more guts than I have. I often wonder if I'll be worth a god-damned when I get out of the army. I know right now I ain't worth the ground to bury me in. I just get run around like you do and don't get anywhere, so you see you aren't alone. I know what little you make helps a lot, so I give you a lot of credit for trying. I'm gonna try to bust this cold, I don't know what with, but I do know without it my morale may get a little above the zero mark.

Wal Rob, I'll say so-long for now, but I'll write again soon. Give my love to Marge and the baby.

Yer Bruther
Rich

P.S. I received your birth announcement

---

68   Richard mentions section eight. This is a term that comes from Section VIII of the World War II-era United States Army Regulation 615-360, which provided for the discharge of those deemed mentally unfit for military service.

Pfc. Richard Nabbe – 32920618
514th (HM) Ord. Co.
A.P.O. 230, c/o P.M.
N.Y.C. N.Y.

Pfc. Robert Nabbe
Motor Center Detach.
2525th Service Unit
So. Post, Ft Meyer
Virginia

In Ever Raining Belgium

November 24, 1944

Dear Rob,

I finally got a letter from you today after quite a lapse of time. For some complicated reason, our mail just doesn't get here very often. I did get quite a few packages here of late though, and one of them was from the Nabbe, Tobin combine[d]. I was very pleased to get Margie's package Rob, mainly because it had a Christmas stocking in it, plus a bunch of incidentals that will be very useful. That "Yo-Yo" I got is about worn out because every Joe in my section had a hold of it at one time or another. It seems that at one time they were all champs so they just want to see if they are still good at it. Hm! Maybe it's the beginning of their second childhood.

You certainly seem to have trouble with your job. Over here I'm yelling like hell cause I can't do anything and over there you are yelling twice as loud cause they are working you to death. Isn't it awful? Wal, chum just keep at it til you are worn to a complete frazzle and then you can sit in Walter Reed Hospital for the duration.

What do you know? It stopped raining for two whole days now. Now instead of rain falling in Germany, its bombs. Our planes have been going over like flocks of geese, so I surmise it's rather warm in Heinieland[69] these cold winter days. I sure hope it doesn't rain any more for awhile, because it sure put the damper on activities here abouts.

I sure wish I was with you Rob to see "Suzie" but that can't be, as you already know. However it won't be long now I hope. Mom and Dot have written to me all about

---

69   Richard uses the pejorative, Heinieland, when speaking of Germany.

your new "diaper user" all right, in fact it seems to be the main topic of conversation. I wish you would make up your mind who she looks like because its hard on my visual senses. I bet when she gets older she won't look like any of you. Ha! Ha! That would be funny.

Don't worry about me sneaking home, cause the whole U.S. will know it when I land. Yeah boy, there will be a lot of noise all right. Wine, women and song will be my middle name for about a month. It sure will be swell to talk to a girl in English again. I can speak pretty good French now. So I get along O.K., but now I'm isolated like a flea on an elephant's ear, so what good does it do me? If I ever get loose again, I'll learn a few words I'll never forget. There is a catch though, where I'm heading, you say "Fraulien" not "Mademoiselle" so now where am I? Also it costs you $64 for even saying "hello" to anyone in German, so maybe I'm better off not to speak at all. Quite a costly conversation eh? Well little chum, that's about all for now, but will write again soon. Keep a lookout for my paltry few letters cause I haven't forgotten you by a long shot.

Yer bruther
Rich

P. S. Regards to Marge and Suzie

Pfc. Richard Nabbe – 32920618
514th (HM) Ord. Co.
A.P.O. 230, c/o P.M. N.Y.C.

Pfc. Robert Nabbe
Motor Center Detach.
2525 Service Unit
So. Post, Ft Meyer
Virginia.

December 19, 1944[70]

Dear Rob,

This isn't exactly what you could call a real letter, but more or less to thank you for your package that arrived yesterday. Please don't say anything, but yours was the most practical package I have received. I assure you I can use all the articles you sent and appreciate them very much. I needed the razor blades, the wash rag (real bad) the comb and mirror, the flash light and all the other stuff too. Believe me it was a real Christmas package. That cigarette pack holder was also a very welcome article.

Your brother is getting the hell scared out of him these days. I'm sure if you read the papers you'll know why. I now live in a cellar, way down under, and am damned glad I am too. The way the bombs and bullets fly around here is a shame. In case you have never been strafed and bombed, I'll tell you how if feels. First off, you don't need to have someone tell you a hienie air force is around, cause about a million bullets of all calibers are greeting his arrival. At night it's real pretty, like six fourth of Julys all rolled into one. So you dive for a cellar or a bomb shelter and run like hell. Then if you are the object of that Hienies mission the fun begins. The plane starts in a dive and you start to sweat, it gets closer and closer and then the guns start to chatter. Boy I'm not fooling Rob, your stomach feels like the size of a golf ball and you just hold on tight. Then when it sounds like he's about to come right in with you, he lets his eggs[71] go. There's a couple seconds elapse before those bombs hit, but believe me it seems like 3 hours. Well the bombs hit, and you think the whole god-damned world is blowing up. The joint rocks

---

70 The Battle of the Bulge, Hitler's last big offensive, took place from December 16, 1944 through January 25, 1945. Richard was in the thick of it.

71 Eggs refer to German bombs.

like a stuck pig and you don't know whether to laugh or cry. Well that one was close, but he missed, so you just wait till he winds up again. Now old Jerry keeps on playing like that, and in a little while he takes off. You look for holes in your posterior, shake the plaster off your blankets and settle down for awhile to try and sleep. Of course you don't get it cause the Hienie only went to get some gas and bombs, but it's a breather between rounds anyway. Be glad you are where you are old boy. Cause it ain't much fun here. It raises hell with my nervous system and it takes a hell of a lot of underwear which I can't get replaced. They better quit before I have to go around naked. Well Rob, I hope you like this blow by blow description of my adventure but it's time for these lights to go out so I'll say so long for now. Many thanks for your sweet package, and I'll be seeing you (I hope) soon.

Your brother
Richie

Pfc. Richard Nabbe – 32920618
514 Ord (HM) Ord Co.
A.P.O. 230 % P.M. N.Y.C.

Motor Center Det.
2525 Service Unit
South Post, Ft. Meyer
Virginia
A.S.N. 32598454

"A La Belgique"

January 4, 1945

Dear Rob,

I guess you must be a bit worried about me cause I haven't written in quite a while. Well to tell you the truth, I have been more than busy these days. It seems our peaceful days are over because the Hienies are raining hell with us over here and letter writing seems sort of far away right now. I haven't had any word from you for a real long time, but to-day I got two letters from you. That the first I had received in three weeks. Mail is scarce as hens tail feathers in molting season, but we have hopes that it will improve in the near future.

We aren't so worried about the Heinie planes as we are the damned buzz bombs.[72]

I received your pictures of Suzie and she sure looks grand. Thanks a lot Rob, I appreciate your thoughtfulness. Tell Marge that the picture of the baby is fine, but she didn't come out so good. Irregardless, I think she looks in fine shape and in good health.

We are having cigarette troubles too these days, we were quite fortunate right along but it seems that for some reason they get scarcer and scarcer each day. I did all right on my Christmas boxes and I don't have to worry for a couple of weeks. I gave a lot away to fellows who just didn't have any, but that's O.K. because I know what its like over here to be without smokes and its tough. You smoke an awful lot here because your

---

72 Buzz bombs--In June 1944, the German army began the use of what would be a
    very unique, very deadly, and historical weapon called the **V1**. The 'V' stood for
    Vergeltungswaffe, which meant "vengeance weapon" but were known to American
    soldiers as "buzz bombs". These flying bombs made a very distinct sound as they
    flew overhead at low altitude, before the timing mechanisms expired. Then, the bomb
    fell to earth, and exploded.

nerves get ragged. Every time a buzz bomb comes over I grab for a weed, so you can see that a carton lasts about two days.

Speaking of turkey, we had a darned good dinner on Christmas and New Years and I'm not kidding either. The Cooks did a swell job on the dinner and it was really fine.

I see you are back to your old traits of robbing the Sec. of Wars paper. My how you get around. Well it saves paper doesn't it.[73]

We left where we were up front, but we almost was mixing up Yankee khaki with Hienie green for awhile. Yeah it was too hot for me out there. I just about ran out of prayers when we retreated. Now we are situated in a lovely place and it is nice. Nine out of ten buzz bombs the Germans send out, land here. To give you an example, I was sleeping in a lady's house between two gorgeous sheets in a beautiful big bed and I thought I hit Shangrila. You know that's quite a change from those holes in the ground we are used to hiding in, when along comes a big buzzeroo and damned near lands in her back yard. Well, I was quite rudely awakened by this canned flying salmon and I wound up laying in the corner. To pour iodine on an open cut, a slab of plaster the size of a server plate come floating down and slapped me right on the noodle. Wal I dragged my beat up carcass out of a pile of glass doors and plaster and started looking for my pants, when in flies the old lady. (No door, it got blown off) and starts yelling about me getting hurt. Well truthfully, I wasn't at all, but I didn't feel so good either. Wal, she tears out of what was left of her house and comes back with a great big bottle of cognac. She leads me to a chair and pours me a neat hooker the size of a water glass and I sipped it down like a man dying from thirst would a thimble of water. When ye olde bottle finally slumped to the floor, there were two dead soldiers and one was me. They could drop a 500 pounder between my legs and I would have slept through it that night. The next day she asked me if I was going to sleep there again that night and I said I was sorry, but I can't stand high altitudes. I now sleep way down deep in another ladies cellar and I like it fine. The deeper the better. That torpedo tore every window on the second floor out,

---

73 Robert explains: "This was a bit of chutzpa on my part. I was sent to the Secretary of War's office for a reason I have forgotten and was pointed to a seat next to his female secretary's desk where she types his correspondence. She went into his office to inform him of my appearance. On her desk was an open box of his personal stationary and I quickly purloined several sheets with the heading, 'Secretary of War'. I thought I'd play a joke on Mom by writing my daily letter to her on this impressive sheet. I recall that I also sent a letter to Richard but I must have had second thoughts about this being photographed for V-MAIL and being traced back to me so I quickly got rid of the paper. I guess I mentioned this to him per his response in his 1/4/45 letter."

sash and all, blew all the doors off, hinges and all and knocked about an acre of plaster off the walls. We spent half the night cleaning up the joint with a shovel. Then she asks if I want to sleep there. Not me bud.

Every time one of those things land it tears up a city block and some nights they came over here like flies chasing a hunk of sugar. Oh me, what have I got to worry about? Just cause my hair stands up like a wire brush doesn't mean anything. Also the god-damned hienie airoplanes keep snooping around and planting eggs all over the place. They better cut it out or I'll be a nervous wreck. Life is rough in the E.T.O.

Well Rob, thanks for your swell letters, and I'll write you again between buzz bombs.

Yer noive shattered bruther
Richie

Regards to the little one and her momma also!!

Pfc. Richard Nabbe – 32920618
514 (H.M.) Ord. Co.
A.P.O 230 % P.M. N.YC.

Pfc. Robert Nabbe
Motor Center Detach.
2525 Service Unit
South Post, Ft. Meyer
Virginia

January 28, 1945

Belgium

Dear Rob,

Here's a line or two to let you know I'm thinking of you. I received a letter from you that was held up by that break through, and I just received it now. I appreciate your thoughtfulness by your placing those beer labels in your letter. Every time I look at them my mouth waters like Niagara Falls. Have you no pity in your soul? I get beer to drink our here once in awhile, but it's just dirty water. All we use if for is to use it for a chaser for cognac. Not that the stuff hasn't enough water in it already. The civilians get two bottles, one full, one empty and equalize the contents into the two and refill them with water. Now at twelve or fourteen dollars a quart it is pretty expensive water. If I was dying on a desert, I could see the point. However all it requires over here to get a drink is to open your mouth as you plow through a snow drift and you get a reasonable facsimile of it.

I got a letter from Joe[74] and he's having quite a time with the heat, while I have to wrap my balls in rabbit fur to keep them from freezing off. It beats the hell out of me. I don't know who to sympathize with, him or me. I guess the States is the happy medium.

Right now I'm pretty safe from those god-damned buzz bombs. They sail around this place too, but they keep on going. That suits me fine. The last joint we were in just about had me nuts. Oh for the peace and quiet of the country. Oh yeah, not over here. I wasn't doing bad, out of ten days, I was drunk 9 and 9/10 nights. Yep, and it didn't cost me a cent either. As the cat said "You have to make calls if you want to get results." Unquote. Right now I'm on a rest cure, the reason is because I can't get out.

---

74 Joe is mostly likely Joe Urban, a family friend.

I'll find a way though!! There's always a way!!

I'm sorry you went on days again Rob, but you should know the army by now. I know, believe me. Well, maybe you'll get that well deserved rest you need. How in the hell do you gain weight with so little sleep. I gain weight too, but it isn't cause I don't get sleep!

I got a letter from the Hertleins and it only took two months to write. I enjoyed it irregardless. They certainly are a pair and are as wacky as ever. I like people that way. I wrote them a letter in return, so I hope they get it.

I'm glad our baby is coming along so well. Margie writes me real often and I get all the info. I like to hear from her too. She's such a swell person, and I'm not fooling either. I have a little pair of shoes I'm sending Susan, and I'm going to paint them myself, so don't say anything! They are those little wooden shoes, and they are cute as hell! This is the fourth pair I've sent now.[75] I hope at least one gets there.

Gee Rob, I'm stuck for conversation right now, so I'm afraid, it's time to quit. The war is coming right along now and it shouldn't last much longer.[76] Take it easy chum, and I'll be seeing you.

Your Bud,
Richie

---

75   Susan's little wooden shoes had her name painted on them.

76   Richard was correct about the war winding down. Germany's Battle of the Bulge offensive failed and by the end of April, Hitler was dead. VE Day—Victory over Europe—occurred on May 8, 1945 when the Germans unconditionally surrendered.

FOLLOWING ORDERS

Another time I went up to Aberdeen Proving Grounds in Maryland where they were having military exercises. The general I was driving wanted me to follow a body of troops through the fields and I said, "Well, sir, this is a road vehicle. This is not a jeep." He said, "Don't argue with me. Just follow those troops." I went cross-country and did I tear up that vehicle! And did I get hell when I got back to the motor pool! I said I was obeying orders. I said I had no choice. I reported that I had informed the general that the car was not for cross-country purposes, but he had insisted we use it that way. I had merely followed orders. I said, "Who am I to disobey a general?"

A FLOODED ROAD

I recall another time when I had to take a general and his wife to White Sulfur Springs in West Virginia. We got out in the country where during wartime most of the roads were empty. The highways had very little traffic and the back roads had none. Usually a dispatcher would route you. They would give you a routing on a map, and you had to follow that because as you needed fuel for your car, you didn't pull up to a gas station. Instead you went to an army post that was usually on the route and you'd get your vehicle serviced and do other things—whatever was necessary.

I was following this route in the Shenandoah Valley and got down into a flooded section of it. When the water deepened, I stopped the car. The general said, "Keep going." And it was with some concern, that I proceeded to go where I was ordered to, not that I *wanted* to. The road was completely under water for about a quarter of a mile. The only way I could tell that I was on the road was by the bushes lining the sides. I aimed down the middle, as there were no other vehicles on it. When I came to little bridges, I knew that as long as I kept the rails on either side, I was on the roadway. I guess the water ran from one to two feet in depth and all the while I was dreading that it was going to stall the engine. But as good fortune would have it, that never happened. And while it looked frightening, it didn't turn out to be as bad as it seemed to be at first.

I finally came up out of the lowland area and back up onto high ground. When I reached that point, there was a state policeman putting a barricade across the road. He said, "Where the devil did you come from?" I replied, "I came the way I'm headed." He said, "This road isn't passable." I said, "That's what I just learned." He asked, "Didn't someone stop you on the other side?" I told him, "There was no one on the other side. There wasn't a car, a vehicle, a barricade or anything—nothing to indicate that this road wasn't passable." He was quite amazed about that.

29 November 1945

RECEIPT

Received from Major W.D. Kelly, Agent Finance Officer

Twenty ——————————00/100——————————Dollars

for expenses incident to a trip to White Sulphur Springs

W.Va. on or about 30 Nov. 1945/

PFC Robert W Nabbe

RECEIPT FOR TRIP TO WHITE SULPHUR
SPRINGS, WEST VIRGINIA, 1945

AN EMBARRASSING MOMENT

I'd been driving for a number of hours and hadn't stopped for any reason. I had to go to the bathroom. When I have to go, I have to go. I was getting pretty desperate and the more uncomfortable one becomes when he needs to go, the less attentive he is to driving safely. As good fortune would have it, we came to a railroad crossing out in the boonies somewhere. A freight train was coming through so I had to stop. Alongside of the track was a little frame railroad structure. I told the general, "Excuse me, sir, I'm going to go out to check the tires on the vehicle." I made a swing around the car and when I got to the back of it, I dashed to the backside of that little structure and relieved myself. It was about as timely as you could get because if I had delayed it any longer, I would have not made it any further.

I walked around the complete building, and as I came to the other side, there was the general's wife doing the same thing I had just finished doing. She was in as much discomfort, I guess, as I had been. I looked at her; she looked at me. Neither one of us said anything. I turned and went back the way I came so I wouldn't have to return to the car alongside of her. I realized the general knew what she was doing out there, and I didn't want him to know that I knew, too.

ICE ON THE SKYLINE DRIVE

We got to White Sulfur Springs, and I offloaded my passengers. I told the dispatcher at the motor pool that I was headed back to Washington. It was a requirement if you had an empty vehicle. If someone needed a lift back to Washington or to the Pentagon, you would drive him. So I wound up with three officers who were returning to Washington. It was in the wintertime, and the air was crisp. It was early winter, though, and the Army-Navy game was on. The officers were listening to the game on the car radio. I wasn't allowed to play the radio. That was a no-no. But if the officers wanted to hear it, it was turned on for them. So I enjoyed the Army-Navy game, too.

I was driving back in the general direction of Front Royal, Virginia paralleling the Skyline Drive, which was up on top of the mountain. When our return route crossed the Skyline Drive, one officer said to me, "How about driving on the Parkway?" I said, "Sure, why not? It's in the direction we're going. There's no problem with that." As we got up to the intersection, we found that the parkway road was barricaded. There were about two inches of snow on the pavement. I said, "Well, it looks like we are not going to be able to do it." The general said, "Sure we are. I'll go out and move the barricade." He and another one of the officers moved it. I steered the car through and they put the barricade back. We drove through a fairyland. I had never seen anything so beautiful. Everything was coated with ice. It looked like crystals, diamond crystals on everything. It was so lovely. I have never in my life seen something that could equal it. At that altitude, I guess the clouds had condensed on the bushes and trees in these fabulous formations. It wasn't like an ice storm; everything was crystallized rather than merely sheathed in ice.

When it came time to come off the parkway, I drove down an exit road. It was then that I could understand why the road had been closed. It was solid ice, and I was slipping and sliding. I had the car in low gear. Using the brakes I could not keep the car under control. I barely kept it on the road. I don't know to this day why I didn't go off the side of the mountain. I started to slide as we were coming up to a tunnel. Icicles had formed across the tunnel like bars on a jail cell. I plunged through that mass of ice—I don't know why I didn't break headlights and windows and everything else—but I burst through the ice. Inside the tunnel a short distance the dry pavement caught my wheels and I was able to brake the car to a stop.

All the officers were saying, "Boy, that was good driving soldier." I had no control over it. It was God's hand on the wheel. I swear it was not anything that I did that kept us from going over the side of the mountain. When I got through to the other side of the tunnel, the road was more passable. Ultimately I reached the bottom and the road was dry again. But for a little while, it was pretty hairy going.

A MYSTERIOUS JOURNEY

I was dispatched on what seemed an ordinary assignment to meet with a captain in an obscure location that had no outward appearance of being a military facility. Furthermore, the vehicle I had been assigned was an equally ordinary dull olive drab passenger car with no distinctive features or insignia other than a few military markings. When I reached the meeting point with the captain, I was quite surprised when he handed me a sidearm to strap on. He was similarly armed, and after backing up to a door in a nondescript building, we loaded the rear trunk of the car with a large quantity of small, unmarked cartons. I had absolutely no clue as to what they contained nor did I venture to ask a superior officer as to the intent or contents of the operation. After completing the loading task we both got into the front seat of the sedan. This was most unusual, as officers without exception rode in the rear of the vehicle. What was equally odd was the captain placing an un-holstered Colt 45 automatic pistol on the seat between us. I never carried a firearm in the normal course of my duties other than when posted on guard duty or guarding prisoners in the stockade, so all this firepower generated a lot of curiosity on my part. A lowly G.I. didn't ask questions especially of a commissioned officer.

We did what we were ordered to do without comment. I was instructed to drive in a normal fashion to Baltimore, Maryland about fifty or so miles from where I had picked up the captain and his cartons. During wartime there was only a limited amount of traffic on the roads, but having been issued a sidearm caused me second thoughts, and I diligently eyed the rear and side-view mirrors more thoroughly than ever. We arrived in the city without incident, and upon instructions from the captain as to where to turn we progressed into a seedy, rundown section of the city with badly neglected streets. Even though I was not driving fast, I hit an unnoticed pothole hard enough to cause the trunk lid to fly open resulting in some of our cargo spilling onto the street. I halted immediately, of course, and with a mad scramble retrieved all the cartons and restored them back in the trunk. Fortunately none of the cartons burst open, and once the captain was satisfied that all were accounted for, we proceeded to our destination in another secondary part of the city, which developed into a mixture of residential and commercial structures that were rundown in appearance. Stopping in front of a garage, we backed in partially and offloaded our cargo.

Once we completed the task, the captain relieved me of my sidearm. He took his own weapon as well as the pistol on the seat and stowed them out of sight. He then proceeded to establish himself in the rear seat as was more customary, and we retraced our steps back to the Military District of Washington.

On the return trip I could barely contain my curiosity but knew it was highly improper to ask any questions. However, I wanted to know the reason for all the firearms, as this was very atypical in the usual course of my duties. Because I was a brazen young man, I took a risk and posed the question. I was surprised when the captain responded. What he told me was quite a shock. He said that the cargo we had just delivered were invasion maps. I wasn't sure if the captain was telling the truth or was putting me on, but if they were, in reality, invasion maps, they could have been for any of a number of areas within the many theaters of war in which our country was involved. I do know there was a high element of security in the assignment, at least from my perspective. Having to be armed left me with the conviction that there must have been some credibility to what the captain said. However, if the maps were not the real thing, the bullets in the pistols surely were.

FIRST-BORN DAUGHTER

Our daughter, Susan, was born during my military service. She arrived on October 18, 1944 and was such a precious addition to my life. Because of my proximity to where Margie and Susan were living, I was able to get home on occasion to watch her development. It was a very good, strong sustaining force for me, not that I had any problems otherwise, but to think of a wife and child waiting for me when this was all over kept me going.

Cpl. Richard Nabbe – 32920618
515 (HM) Ord. Co.
A.P.O. 230 %P.M.N.Y.C.

Pfc. Robert Nabbe
Motor Center Detach.
2525 Service Unit
So. Post, Ft. Meyer
VIRGINIA

France

February 20, 1945

Dear Rob,

I received four letters from you today and believe me it's wonderful to hear from you again. I haven't had mail since God knows when, and my existence here is so dull that I can't compare it with anything.

I'd like to apologize to you in a way, for a letter I sent to mom, in which I told her that I hadn't heard from you in so long, that maybe you couldn't find time to drop me a line. Actually I should know better, cause you are one of my most consistent writers and also I might add most morale up holding. It just seems to get you when you don't get a letter for weeks after weeks. I also realize that I'm the one who is letting you down, but I guess you realize that there are times when it's utterly impossible. I know you never complain, but you have been so swell about it all that I thought I might try and explain a little bit. I swear I'll do better in the future bar all my troubles. In one of your letters, you said that you may get three months off to work on civilian jobs. Well Rob, I certainly hope you get it, cause it will mean that it's three months less you will not have to worry about the Infantry. All I can say is stay away from it if you can. I know, I had over five months of infantry, and it's lousy. They need men all right, and I guess you know why. These Germans aren't exactly pushovers, in fact, they are tough as hell. They are good soldiers and know how to fight. We need men here and need them real bad. In fact, the army is taking men out of Ordnance companies over here for front line duty, so you know they are hard up. I don't know why they don't take those damned S.O.S. troops over here and let them have a dose of what war is like. Well there have been times when I was almost a combination Ord. and infantry soldier, so I guess I can stand it.

Right now I have a good chance of getting hooked and don't think we don't know it. If I do get hooked you'll hear about it, but up till that time, don't mention it to Mom, or even worry about it.[77] *Just stay away Rob, that's all. The only way heros are made is because they have to be, and then if they are a hero, its only because they are lucky to be alive. I ain't no hero and as far as I'm concerned I don't want to be. Let's drop that unsavory subject.*

Here are the answer to your questions in your letters. Pay attention old bean and maybe you can figure it out. #1. Yes, I did, and it wasn't a darned bit funny either. #2. Yes, after a while it got so hot, we had to. However it would have suited me fine if they would have made up their minds a little sooner. #3. Yes, rest at ease Rob, all goes well. #4. No, none what so ever. #5 Miraculously no. And if I do, I'll promise to let you know. That would answer what you wanted to know Rob.[78] *At least for the present. It's also wonderful the way you folks plug for me and believe me. I'm sincerely grateful from the bottom of my heart. Tell everyone that its more than a pleasure to know such fine people.*

Say Rob, that was swell of you to get that picture blown up of me, I realize you had an awful little picture to work from, but you did a wonderful job of it. That picture was taken right before my Nazi friends paid us a visit. An unwelcome one at that.

I wrote before that I received Susan's pictures and they were swell. Everyone writes me about your baby, and there isn't one that doesn't rave about her. I feel as though I know her since she was born. She did remarkable well on Christmas and that's fine. Sorry I wasn't a contributor, but my day shall come. I get quite a few letters from Marge and so you see I get all the low down. You are lucky to have such a swell family. You got a wonderful wife and a lovely girl. From what Marge tells me you must be real happy. You can believe me Rob, it also makes me happy.

I thought I told you about Mildred and me, but I guess it has gotten by some how. Well chum, here's to the low down! Yes I'm going with her steady again, as a matter of fact, its been many months now. As a matter of fact, I intend to marry her when I

---

77   It was common for men to share with other men the realities of war, while downplaying the seriousness for women, particularly their mothers.

78   Robert's questions to Richard were these: 1. Did you get caught in the invasion? 2. Did you retreat to a safer area and did you get pushed into fighting? 3. Are you comparatively safe now? 4. Are you doing combat work? 5. Have you been wounded? The questions are on a separate piece of paper that Robert later tucked inside Richard's letter after he received it so that he could remember what he had asked knowing that Richard would not be able to answer in any way that would give away army secrets. This was a way to for Richard to avoid censor removing what he had written.

get home, and that's no idle talk. I guess you think I'm hasty, but believe me I'm not. Mickey and I have been writing steady to each other for the last eight months and we have everything straightened out to a very decisive point. You know Rob, I learned a lot of things since I have been in the army and she was one that I straightened out. I guess you thought when I left here, I had forgotten all about her. Well I didn't, I never forgot her at all. Even in Alberdeen I had her on my mind, its just one of those things. Well I never told anyone about it, and at the time we were trying to see how much we could make each other hate each other, so I decided the best thing to do was just let it go at that. Well one day in Seresy Forrest I made up my mind to write to her. You don't realize what a lot of things you can think up when you had a lot of time on your hands. Well we had lots of time, so I sat in my little fox hole and did just that. I finally realized what a lot of mistakes I had made and even had myself ashamed. So, I wrote to her. It was just a friendly letter and wasn't meant to state anything. In fact, I didn't even expect an answer. However, I did after a while and as I expected it was just a nice conversational letter about common things. However at the end of it, she said she had something to tell me and if it was O.K. by me, to write and tell her if I wanted to hear it. So naturally, I did just that. I was quite curios. Well I did get a reply a few weeks later and to my surprise it was just like the previous one, just ordinary conversation. Well in the last paragraph, as if you had cut the rest of the letter off completely she said that she still loved me and never cared about anyone else and that I needn't bother answering the letter if I didn't care to. Well I did care to so I answered it but quick. I told her exactly what I thought and the preceding letter answered all my questions. I asked if she would be willing to go back with me again, and she said she did, so now we are all straightened out. I have an entirely new slant on things and so has she. We get along remarkably fine despite the fact that there is only a few thousand miles between us. I think we have everything under control. I can tell she's not a kid any longer and all those silly ideas she used to have, faded, just like I expected. So that's that, I'm carrying on my romance by mail, but I sure would like to do it in person. Oh baby!!

I haven't asked her to marry me, cause things are so uncertain, but if I ever get a chance, I will, but quickly. I've nothing to offer her as you probably know, but maybe I can fix that up too. Keep this under you lid chum. I know you aren't a chatterbox but I ain't out of this mess yet, and the way things happen, it doesn't pay to advertise. Of course you're my brother and I can tell you anything, but you know how some people are! (I don't mean you).[79]

I guess that answers another question for you Rob. Well I guess this letter will hold

---

79   Robert stated that he urged his brother not to get married quickly after returning
        from war. Richard chose to ignore this advice.

you for a bit, so I must say so long for now. Give my regards to Marge and Suzy, and take care of yourself, brothers like you are sort of hard to replace these days.
    Yer bruther
    Richie

    P.S. I got a letter from Joe and he's O.K.

Cpl. Richard Nabbe – 32920618
514 Ord. HM Co.
A.P.O. 230 %PM.N.Y.C.

Pfc. Robert Nabbe
Motor Center Detach.
2525ᵗʰ Service Unit
So. Post, Vt. Meyer
Virginia

Belgium

March 5, 1945

Dear Rob,

Well chum, I received about five more letters from you, all centered around New Years. You can see how badly screwed up the mail is cause I got some you wrote after that. Irregardless, I certainly enjoyed each and every one of them and I'll try to make some sort of a reply in this letter.

The weather seems to be holding out pretty good here of late. In spite of the occasional rain we have, I can stand it. The lack of snow is just wonderful. Soon it should be spring and I'll certainly welcome the warm weather. I bet it's a lot colder back home now than it is here.

Well you can stop worrying about me Rob, cause I'm away behind the lines again. The buzz bombs have ceased to come over and all fronts here are pushing like hell.[80] This war can't last much longer now. I got some swell pictures in Stovelos and if they come out, I'll send them to you. I sure hope they do, cause I really want those pictures. Boy, I'd give my right arm to have a good camera. I missed most of all the good pictures, but there are still some good material. If you can get a hold of any no. 4 contact paper, I'd appreciate it if you would send it right along. That's the only stuff we can get any decent print from. It's always so misty around here that pictures seldom come out good.

Thanks a lot of the things you are sending me Rob. I can certainly use it. I haven't received any of them to date, but I should pretty soon. I did get my sweater that Mom

---

80 Richard survived the major German offensive, the Battle of the Bulge, which lasted
    from December 16, 1944 through January 25, 1945.

sent me and it sure is warm. I was afraid I would be in the warm months by the time I received it.

I didn't want to worry you folks during that break through, but we were so busy that I didn't even try. Right now its peaceful, and I can think back to those days not so long ago. I'm glad I don't have to go through that again. I wrote you a letter right after we got visited by the Germans in general and I know how Francis Scott Key felt like when he wrote the "stars Spangled Banner". Well it all passes by Rob, and it also brings us that much nearer to the end of the war. That's a lot to look forward to. Gosh but I've about forgotten what its like to fish or hunt again. I don't know what I'd give to go on an old fashioned picnic again up at Califon. Well kid come the end of the war, we'll see what cooks. I hope you made that factory deal old boy. That will make things in general a lot easier. That a boy, just stay away from the old infantry. That is all that I ask of you. You seem to be so screwed up on your deals lately. I didn't know what to expect. Do you work nights or days? Let me know how that factory deal comes out, will you?

You never saw such a mess in all your life as was the town on Bastogne. That place is strewn all over with all kinds of equipment of all kinds. A lot of guys died during that deal. I didn't miss getting hung up there myself by very much. Oh me, such as to war.

Things seem a bit monotonous around here, I have half a mind to wish I was back up at the front. This continual quiet gets on my nerves. I sure have a changeable mind haven't I? Well you take about nine months of chasing the Hienies and then practically get slapped in the S.O.S, it gets you down. Well the Army is funny, here today and gone tomorrow. I sure do hope to be writing from Germany before long.

Well Rob, that's it for now. I realize this isn't much, but it helps a little. Thanks again, and give my regards to the little mite and her mama.

Yer brother,
Richie

Cpl. Richard Nabbe – 32920618
514ᵗʰ (HM) Ord. Co.
A.P.O. 230 % P.M. NYC.

Pfc. Robert Nabbe
Motor Center Detach.
2525 Service Unit
So. Post, Fort Meyer
Virginia

Germany[81]

March 10, 1945

Dear Rob,

Don't feel bad if you can't write to me for a few days or a week. Hell I don't expect you to write all the time, you do well enough as it is. I'm glad your furlough was a success, get all the time home cause you'll surely appreciate it later on. I received a letter from Mom with a few pictures of the baby and she sure is an adorable little baby. She sure is cute all right, and those pictures of Mom sure have a tendency to make one awfully homesick. Pap's lunch room[82] looks to me like a real nice prospect. I've got a premonition that if it works out, he'll quit his job and go down there steady. You know that was always on his mind and I don't doubt that it's the goal he's trying to attain. I hope it does work out, all will be better for him if it does.

Thanks for the offer Rob, but I don't need anything at the present time. As far as soap, razor blades, toothpowder and etc, goes, I can usually get all I need, so it won't be necessary to send any of those. Say if you see that no good J.H.[83], you tell him I'm still

---

81   In the actual letter, the word, "Germany", at the top of the letter is bordered on each side by swastikas that Richard drew to show he is in enemy territory. It also means the Allies have advanced into Germany.

82   "Pap's lunchroom" came to fruition. Fred and Edna, Robert and Richard's parents, opened a restaurant on the Jersey Shore. Fred worked all week in Northern New Jersey while Edna and Dorothy ran the restaurant. He joined them on the weekends. Most of the customers were local fishermen. Robert recalled that his father used to complain that Edna used too much meat in the hamburgers and urged her to use less. The restaurant was a success. Fred and Edna ran it for a few years and then moved to Florida in 1950 after Robert and Marjorie relocated there in 1949.

83   J.H. is Jimmy Horahan, a family friend from Irvington, NJ.

waiting for that letter from him. What a buddy he is. I know what's wrong with him he just don't like to write.

Your brudder was clerking for a while, but he ain't anymore. Yep, I'm back to work again. Oh well, I was getting too fat anyway. I'm up around 190 lbs as it is. I wish I could lose ten or fifteen of it. I've got a funny feeling I'm liable to.

This land called Germany is in quite a sad condition, or at least what I've seen it is. Boy they sure knocked hell out of everything. There isn't anything that's worth picking up from Belgium to the Rhine River. All that's left is dust and bricks. That's the way I like it, I hope the rest of the damned German country gets the same dose. Those bastards are paying now and it's a pretty expensive installment believe me.[84] Don't be surprised if the war ends one of these days. There isn't a hell of a lot left for them to fight with.

Well, brudder mine, that's all the idle chatter floating around this eve, so I shall bid you adieu. Take care and stay sober.

Your brother
Richie

P.S. Stay away from the infantry.[85]

---

84   Throughout the letters Richard speaks harshly of Germany though his grandparents emigrated from there to the USA in the late 1800s. While Richard and Robert's father, Fred, was born in the United States, Fred's older brother was born in Berlin. Robert stated that Fred would berate his father for speaking German, telling him, "Speak English. You're an American now." Many American soldiers were of recent German descent but it didn't stop them from seeing the Germans as a purely evil enemy.

85   Richard continuously tells his brother to stay away from the infantry. Richard knew from direct experience the hell of war and did not want his older brother involved in it.

Cpl. Richard Nabbe – 32920618
514th H.M. Ord Co
A.P.O. 230 % P. M. N.Y.C.

Pfc Robert Nabbe
Motor Center Detach.
2525th Service Unit
S. Post, Ft. Meyer
Virginia

Germany

March 15, 1945

Dear Rob,

Well Rob, I received the package you mentioned in your previous letter. I also received three small packages with the sardines and chocolates. I swear I don't know where you think up your ideas, but you can believe me, that I more than appreciate those little things you do send. I got your lighter and also the picture holders. Both are quite satisfactory. I'm sorry I said I didn't need toilet articles, but the ones you sent will get used all right. You hit my favorite shaving cream right on the noodle, so you see it wasn't all in vain by any means.

I received a couple letters from you, dated December fourth and also a card. You can just see how mail goes here. Well I enjoyed them just as much as a really recent one, so don't you worry Rob. That Merry Christmas drawing on the back of one of your letters is really good and I'm saving it as an example of my brothers' art. You are still good at it you know?[86] Also, thanks for your valentine, your verses are exceptionally original and I sure hope they prove to be true.

It's been truly beautiful here for the last few days. Just like summer. It sure seems strange to see the sun shine for more than five minutes at a time. They got me working pretty hard, but I don't mind it, especially with such fine weather.

I know this isn't much of a letter Rob, but at least it's a couple lines to let you know I'm all right.

---

86 Richard mentions Robert's artistic ability. After the war, Robert attended art school at the Newark School of Fine and Industrial Arts using money from the G.I. Bill to pay his tuition. Extremely talented, Robert painted many oils and watercolors, all of which have been preserved by the family.

O lack of day and joy!! I won't go into the infantry! My eyes are too bad so they won't take me. Now if they won't take me, I know darned well that they won't take you. They may fill you full of that old horse shit, but don't worry kid, the only sight you'll ever look down is that jalopy you are trying to strew all over Washington.

Wal brudder mine, that's it, so stay a little sober, at least till I can get there to help you get plastered.

Old South Pacific bound[87]
Richie

---

87   As the war is winding down in Germany, Richard believes he will be sent to the South Pacific to fight the Japanese. He was not.

Cpl. Richard Nabbe – 32920618
514th H.M. Ord. Co.
A.P.O. 230 %PM. N.Y.C.

Pfc. Robert Nabbe
Motor Center Det.
2525th Service Unit
So. Post Ft. Meyer
Virginia

Germany

March 20, 1945

Dear Robbie,

Greetings my boy, and how are all the miseries of life nibbling at your tortured soul these days? Oh they all have full stomachs, eh? Tsk. Tsk. I bet you are a mere shadow of your shadow. Well from the sound of your letters and those from your lovely wife, I could say you are doing pretty well, and despite the few petty ironies of life, you are leading a rather happy existence. That's the way Rob, you keep an eye on the home front and keep all the gears running smoothly.

I received the photos of Suzie and she certainly is a ray of ultra violet in any ones life. All kidding aside, she's adorable and she looks like you too. I hope Margie doesn't read this. Well she does Rob, and besides, she has to look like somebody. She has finally gotten to the stage of looking like a young lady now and I'll but she'll be real purty when she gets older. Thanks old boy, I really appreciate those pictures.

I also received your two small packages you sent. They contained a wash cloth, towel, and handkerchiefs. All accounted for? You are a man after my own heart Rob. I can use those articles very much. Things of that nature are very scarce around here, if not nonexistent. No need to tell you how much I thank you for them Rob. Regardless as to how trivial it may seem to you, they certainly mean an awful lot to me. I suppose this is like biting the hand that feeds you, but I would like to make a request from you. I would like to have a couple of "T" shirts if it's at all possible. You know they are like the ones I had with Aberdeen printed on them. In fact, if you look through my junk at home, you might find a couple and they would do just as well as new ones. We use them for underwear tops and they are a lot nicer. If you get around to that chum, I shall more than appreciate it.

Wow, I'm tired and I'm not fooling. We are pretty busy these days and they keep us going right along. Well that's what we're here for so I shouldn't kick. All is quite peaceful around these parts, which suits me fine. Maybe we'll be moving up soon. I hope so, I get tired of this monotony. If it ain't one thing, it's another. Well Rob here where I say g'nite for now, so I'll say so long and many thanks again.

Your brother
Richie

P.S. Regards to you know who

PLEASURES OF SUMMER

Aside from the duties I had to perform, there are other little incidents that I recall with some pleasure. Washington is a very hot, humid town. It gets really sticky. The humidity is more intense than Florida. It's quite uncomfortable in Washington in the summer. The nation's capital had an extensive trolley system. I don't know why the city ever gave it up because it was very efficient. One run started somewhere in Washington and went to Georgetown. It ran along the banks of the old Chesapeake and Ohio Canal and above the Potomac River to an amusement park called Glen Echo and beyond that to a place called Cabin John. This line ran through the woods. I would say that only about ten percent of the length of it was actually in an urban area. The rest of it was rural. Of course it didn't get a big play or much use. The line was just run in the summer time for the most part because it connected with Glen Echo Amusement Park, which closed after the summer season ended. But while the trolley was in operation we used to get aboard that thing and ride to the end of the line. And the motorman, for the most part, would open up that front windshield and the air would just rush through. It was like air conditioning. It was so delightful to get relief from the heat. I'd ride to the end of the line and turn around and come back. It would take about an hour altogether and it was one way of spending a cool hour for about a dime's worth of expense.

Another one of the things that I enjoyed on my off-duty hours in the summer when it was so hot was this: Usually another G.I. and I would walk way, way, way up the Potomac River on the Virginia side—almost to Potomac Falls. We'd make a raft by just taking some driftwood and interweaving it together. We'd take our clothes off—we had bathing suits, of course—and keeping our uniforms out of the water on the raft, we'd float all the way down the Potomac River, practically back to Washington. The river was clean. It was a good, clean stream back in those days. The rafting trip was just so delightful. It was pleasant to enjoy a summery day cost free by floating down that river. Best of all, we'd stay nice and cool. I did that any number of times when the opportunity allowed. On the riverfront, down on what they called Maine Street, there were some excursion boats that would paddle around out in the Potomac. For fifty cents you could get on one of those. That was another way of staying cool.

Staying in the barracks in the summer time was beastly. They were not cool. They had no screens on the windows and if the windows were open, we had the bugs. So getting out in the evening in the summer to escape the heat was always a challenge. But I always managed to do something that was pleasurable in my efforts to get cool.

COUSIN LORRAINE

During the course of my military experience, I had a second occasion to meet a cousin, Uncle Horace's daughter, Lorraine. Her husband was a Navy man—in fact, he was a career Navy man. Somehow or another he got assigned to Washington. I hadn't seen Lorraine since we were little children. I guess I was three or four years old the last time I had seen her. How she ever found out I was in the Washington area, I don't know. But she wrote me a letter and said that her husband was going to be temporarily assigned there. She asked if could I find her an apartment. During the war there just weren't any apartments available in Washington. But as good fortune would have it, a friend of mine who was married was shipping out. His wife was going to go back to live with her folks, and he had a lease on an apartment that he couldn't get out of. He told me that if my cousin wanted that apartment, he'd sublease it to her just to get out from underneath the rental agreement. I wrote to Lorraine and said that I had a place for her. I gave her the particulars and she got herself established there.

Ultimately, Lorraine called me, and I went out to visit with her. They were over in Anacosta where the Naval base was located, so her husband wasn't too far from his duty station. I looked the apartment over and thought it was a pretty good one. As far as I could see, it was accommodating. But Lorraine wasn't happy there for some reason. She moaned and groaned about that apartment, and I thought to myself, "Lady, if you could only know how hard it is to find any kind of a place to live in Washington during this war period, you'd be satisfied." She never was very appreciative of my efforts.

I also saw two of my other cousins during my time in D.C. I had a call from Uncle George's daughters. My cousins, Alice and Carol, were in Washington for one reason or another and contacted me, so I met with them. We went out to dinner together one evening. So, surprisingly, while I was in the army I saw four of my cousins. That's what I keep saying about the world being so small. Honestly, you can hardly go anywhere without running across someone you know or know of.

A PRANK IN THE WHITE HOUSE

Eventually I was assigned to the White House proper. I mean I actually was in the White House as a chauffeur. While I was detached from my other duty, I was temporarily assigned to the White House. There was no chauffeur's room so the drivers were established in President Roosevelt's office on the lower floor. This was his private office, the one from which he gave his Fireside Chats. The Oval Office was upstairs. Right close by was the swimming pool that had been installed for his use. The proximity of the office to the swimming pool allowed Roosevelt to move easily by wheelchair to the pool, as swimming was a form of physical therapy for him. The paneled room was interesting and was decorated with President Roosevelt's collection of ship models. Also on display were opalescent bottles that had been dredged up from New York harbor. The British Navy during the Revolutionary War had left the bottles when they had taken over Manhattan and patrolled the harbor.

One day while I was waiting to be assigned, I sat in Roosevelt's chair, and I put my feet up on his desk. My companion was horrified and was sure that I would be sent to jail for this misdeed. I said to him, "I want you to know that you can actually say you saw somebody who sat in the highest chair of the land, in the seat of the President of the United States. His name is Robert W. Nabbe." I look upon that as very amusing. It was at a point when I was a very brash and blasé young man. By that time I had been exposed to so many dignitaries that they all looked quite ordinary to me.

CHAUFFEURING THE GENERALS

I ultimately got assigned to chauffeur only the highest level of General Officers. One of the people whom I remember with great fondness whom I chauffeured on occasion was Omar Bradley. He was called a soldier's general. He was just that type of a person. General Bradley was very mild mannered, very dignified. He just commanded respect automatically. He was probably one of the greater leaders of the world without all the publicity that attended it.

I have admitted to a certain level of brashness due partly to my youth and partly to having been thrust into the midst of the central point of our war efforts in both the Pentagon and Washington, D.C. Seeing so many high-level military and civilian personages became rather ordinary, and while I fully respected our leaders, I was no longer in awe. I recall one instance when I was dispatched to pick up a General Officer at his home. The trip ticket did not indicate a name, just a destination. When I arrived at the residence I rang to inform of my presence and that the car was awaiting.

A rather pleasant gray-haired man in civilian clothing answered the door and I asked, "Hi, Pops. Is the general ready?" He indicated that it would be a few minutes and to come in and wait. When I entered the living room I saw a framed photo on a table of the general I was to chauffeur and much to my horror saw that it was the same person who had admitted me. The pleasant gray-haired man was General Omar Bradley himself. I felt quite foolish, but General Bradley was such a refined gentleman he never mentioned my faux pas.

Later in the war I drove General Bradley on a number of future occasions when he was stateside. He was quite instrumental in our European invasion so was abroad much of the time. The last time I chauffeured for him was a jaunt to the White House where he was meeting with President Roosevelt. I remember the photographers taking his photo as he exited the vehicle with me holding open the door and saluting. Somewhere in some dusty archives this photo may be buried. Omar Bradley was a soldier's soldier and a much beloved and highly regarded man by all ranks and files down to the footslogging infantryman. I certainly held him in equal esteem.

Washington, D. C.
17 November 1945

Received from Major W. D. Kelly, QMC, War Departmrnt Motor Center,
The Pentagon, Washington, D. C. the sum of twenty dollars $20,00) for
use in connection with a trip to Uniontown, Penna.

ROBERT W. NABBE
Pfc. Motor Center Det.
Hq. Co., War Dept.

RECEIPT FOR TRIP TO UNIONTOWN, PENNSYLVANIA, 1945

Washington, D. C.
17 November 1945

Received from Major W. D. Kelly, QMC, War Department Motor Center,
The Pentagon, Washington, D. C. one (1) book of U. S. Government Tax
Exemption Certificates Nos. W-262,245 to 262, 250 for use in connection
with an official trip to Uniontown, Pennz.

Robert W. Nabbe
Pfc. Motor Center Det.
Hq. Co., War Dept.

RECEIPT FOR BOOK OF TAX EXEMPTION CERTIFICATES, 1945

A TRAIN GOES AWRY

I was on duty on the second shift at the C Street Garage when I was dispatched to pick up a general in an unfamiliar location. I had a comprehensive knowledge of the city by this time and most of my passengers were picked up or delivered to the more typical facilities within the Military District of Washington. In this instance, I was directed to a pick up point that was not only unfamiliar but also a bit bizarre once I arrived at it.

I cannot recall all the particular alleys, passageways, and corridors that I had to negotiate with my limousine. I do remember having a rather difficult time reaching the pickup point at the inner recesses of the Treasury Building. It was there that I, at long last, emerged into a hidden courtyard containing a railroad spur. There was a brick wall about eight feet in height enclosing the area with the railroad tracks dead ending at the rearmost point of the wall. At a later time, after this incident, I was able to pin point the exterior location of the wall and noted that it was about twelve feet above street grade. I cannot recall a railroad spur running on surface streets in this area and conclude the tracks ran underground to emerge at the rear of the building. It all seemed highly secretive and most likely was.

I parked the limousine near the tracks and before long a string of passenger cars came slowly, backing out of an obscure darkened passageway. It was about eleven p.m. and the area was only dimly illuminated. The general was in one of the cars, and fortunately for him, not in the rearmost one as the train kept coming backwards without any lessening of motion or evidence of braking. I was standing by my vehicle and watched in astonishment as the train continued to back up until it reached the end of the track. The last coach rammed into the brick wall. I guess the engineer felt the impact and stopped the train but not before the coach was projecting over the street. Being wartime and with little or no automotive traffic at that late hour, it appeared that the only thing injured was the engineer's pride. There was a huge shower of bricks raining down on the street but fortunately no cars were parked at the curb and no pedestrians afoot to witness the mishap.

I watched all of this transpire as if in slow motion or as in a dream where you can see what's happening but are powerless to do anything about it. I can't recall any railroad crewmember signaling the train as it backed up or anyone else controlling the train's progress in the courtyard. In spite of the dramatic mishap, it appears there was no immediate confusion or concern so I rounded up my general and took him to his destination.

I never saw mention of this incident in the *Washington Post* or heard any feedback within the command, and I was never questioned as an eyewitness. Apparently the whole thing was kept hushed up, but no one ever told me not to discuss it. During my wartime service I was careful not to divulge anything I saw or did unless requested to do so by a superior officer. I was rather amused by the whole incident but kept it to myself until this accounting.

CHAUFFEURING CLARK, MARSHALL, AND EISENHOWER

I don't mean to say that I didn't respect the generals or regard them highly for what they had achieved, but there were a few who I didn't think too highly of. General Mark Clark was somebody I chauffeured that I did not like at all. I found him to be arrogant and condescending. I also didn't much care for George Marshall for the same reasons. These were tough men and they were military and unemotional. I can understand the reason for their being that way with their awesome responsibilities.

I chauffeured General Dwight D. Eisenhower, but only when he was in the United States. Eisenhower was a man who had this deep humility, a very deep humility. He didn't think himself as a great man. That I knew because I drove him frequently and got to know him well. I was with the general and Mrs. Eisenhower any number of times and spent quite a bit of road time with them both. I don't mean social time, but on the road driving them. I watched them interact with other people. I drove the Eisenhowers to Congress. I took them to dinners. I also took them to social functions.

EISENHOWER'S KINDNESS

One time during a heavy snowfall I drove General Eisenhower to a social function given by General Montgomery or Mountbatten—I don't remember which British leader it was. The British officer was temporarily established in a magnificent home that was perched right on a cliff overlooking the falls of the Potomac River. The house had a huge, glassed-in observation room. When we got there, this British dignitary—Montgomery or Mountbatten—greeted General Eisenhower at the door. He said, "Your man can use the stables." Eisenhower said, "My man? My driver comes in the house and I want him fed." That's the way Eisenhower was. He thought of his troops first. In any event, I was escorted into this room overlooking the falls and a British butler came in and asked me what I would like. I said, "Well, whatever . . . a dinner, a bottle of beer." He hustled around and got my food. It was amazing to me that I was treated with such consideration because the Brits didn't treat their underlings or subordinates like that at all. They treated them like servants, whereas, Eisenhower did not treat people that way.

A friend of mine named Robert Bishoff from New Jersey was also Eisenhower's chauffeur in the states. Later Bishoff was sent overseas, and for a time we corresponded. In one letter Bishoff told me that while Eisenhower was reviewing troops somewhere in the European Theater, he spotted Bishoff and recognized him as having been his chauffeur stateside. Eisenhower went over and shook Robert Bishoff's hand and asked him how he was doing. He then invited Bishoff to dinner that evening. That's the way this chap reported the incident to me, which just gives another dimension to Eisenhower's humility and his appreciation of the ordinary people. He came from ordinary roots himself.

HONORING GENERAL EISENHOWER

Eisenhower had his own big limousine—siren, red lights, all of it. I had the pleasure of using the siren once or twice. It was really thrilling. But for the most part, Eisenhower didn't want that. He had a five-star plate on his car and it was always covered unless he was in it. Half the time, he wouldn't even let me take the cover off it. He just didn't want that recognition. One time I drove General Eisenhower to a dinner at the Mayflower Hotel. This time, I had the cover off of the five-star plate. We pulled up in front of the hotel. When the general got out, the people, recognizing the big car and then seeing the five stars and then recognizing Eisenhower, just stood around. As I opened the door for him and Eisenhower got out of the car everyone applauded. They clapped very quietly, not loud hoorays or cheers or anything, just a very quiet, dignified applause. Then when he came out from the dinner a little while later, Eisenhower got into the backseat of the car and said to his companion, "Aren't people wonderful." Eisenhower didn't say *he* was wonderful, he said that people were.

A STUDY IN CONTRAST: ONE STRIPE AND FIVE STARS

I wish to qualify that I was not specifically designated as General Eisenhower's personal chauffeur. I had risen in experience within the Pentagon-based Motor Pool of the War Department having gained an extensive knowledge of the principal military facilities within and without the Military District of Washington. With this background I was appointed as a General Officer Chauffeur after about two years of common driving duties on all sorts of assignments and equipment. I was further issued a large limousine for use in driving General Officers. It was a new Packard sedan painted in a glossy olive green under my full control and responsibility for maintenance.

When General Eisenhower was in Washington and/or at the Pentagon in the later stages of the war, I was selected to be his driver. I assume his fulltime chauffeur, Sgt. Kay Somersby, WAC, remained at his London headquarters. Otherwise, she would have seen to his personal transportation when stateside. I was made available to General Eisenhower on an infrequent basis, but remained principally assigned to driving other high-ranking generals on a daily and sometimes nightly basis. I do not recall, however, knowing of any other driver being used as General Eisenhower's stateside chauffeur although it could have been possible as we operated the Motor Pool on a twenty-four-a-day basis.

When I was assigned to General Eisenhower, I was given a large Cadillac limousine that was painted in the standard dull olive green military fashion. It had a five-star plate on the front that was covered when the vehicle was not in use. On the occasions I drove the general, I would remove the cover, but I do recall incidents when he requested that I not remove it. The Cadillac also had a siren activated by a pressure button on the floor. One time while going down Constitution Avenue, I accidentally set the siren to wailing. General Eisenhower told me to turn it off immediately. I indicated that I had accidentally hit the floor switch and apologized. I know from my times with him that undue attention was something he preferred to avoid if possible. Whenever I came to a stop and the public saw the five-star insignia, they would greet General Eisenhower with polite applause just as they had at the Mayflower Hotel.

I recall that when I was called from the chauffeur room to bring up the general's vehicle, I was also instructed to use the private elevator that went from the below-ground level of the Pentagon Motor Pool Garage to the Office of the Chief of Staff in order to escort General Eisenhower to the waiting car. I guess not many people shared his company on a one-on-one basis even if only for a very brief time in the elevator. What was my solemn military duty back then never impacted me at the time as I had been exposed to most of the upper echelon of officers in the army and other branches of the service. As I look back now, I can see that I was given a position of great honor and responsibility to see to the safe delivery to his destination of this very important man.

As I have mentioned elsewhere, I was a young and somewhat brash civilian soldier without ever recognizing that even little cogs have a contribution to make in the vast machinery of global war. I now stand in awe and am grateful for the confidence bestowed upon me as a mere Private First Class. It was immediately after my first stint of driving General Eisenhower that I earned a second stripe, and I somewhat suspect that he may have had a hand in my promotion.

General Eisenhower forwarded to me an autographed photo of himself after that last time I drove him. I have given the photo to my daughter, Susan, because she was born during the time I was the general's driver. I also remember a time that I took Eisenhower and two other generals to the capitol where Eisenhower was to give a speech. As we neared the building, he remarked that he had run out of cigarettes. I was always privy to conversations when I drove high-ranking officers, as the rear-seating compartment wasn't glassed in with a privacy screen. Having an extra pack of Lucky Strikes on me, I passed them onto General Eisenhower who thanked me. He said he would pay me back the next time I drove him, but that was the last time I had the privilege of being his chauffeur. The fortunes of war are strange, indeed.

GENERAL PATTON

While I was at the White House, George Patton showed up with his pearl handled pistols, holsters and all. Patton got the job done; you've got to give the guy credit for that. He was a hard driver, an exhibitionist, and I guess, a showman. He was a whole bunch of things. But one thing for sure, he was a fighter. I didn't chauffeur for Patton; someone else did. I never did get to know Patton other than just seeing his comings and goings at the White House.

OTHER OFFICERS

I can't recall all of the people that came in and out of the White House while I was there. Neither can I remember the various people who passed through the Pentagon, but there were a bunch of them. The Pentagon was the clearinghouse for all of the top military whether the army, navy, marine or air corps. They all passed by me at one time or another. Many of them I remember and recognize. Anything with less than four stars I hardly paid any attention to. A lieutenant general, major general, or a brigadier general seemed to be low ratings after I had been exposed to all the higher-ranking officers. These were commonplace for me, just like the guy at the stage door who sees all the stars coming out the back way.

UNPRODUCTIVE PHOTO OPS

Because of our exposure in driving high-profile people, the Motor Center Detachment of the War Department Motor Pool was issued extra dress or Class A uniforms. We had a daily inspection for neatness and proper attire, well-shined shoes, proper haircuts, and a daily close shave. Our colonel with his staff conducted the inspection noting any small infractions. It was a rigid ritual, but I can see where it was a necessary one, as no high-ranking officer would have tolerated a driver with a sloppy appearance. Officers and drivers alike were highly visible within the very heart of our vast war machine that demanded the highest degree of appearance and confidence at every level of personnel. This was in direct contrast to those under field conditions in the thick of battles abroad who I could safely assume would have gladly exchanged places with those of us at this "elite" level of military service with all its spit and polish.

I was an ordinary G.I., but proud of my uniform and what it represented. I did not need the threat of extra duty as punishment for not measuring up to the colonel's demanding standards. My brass was polished daily, as were my shoes. My uniform was always hand pressed with an iron I had gotten from my Aunt Carrie when I had been home on a brief leave. The latrine end of the barracks was equipped with laundry tubs, scrub boards, yellow soap, G.I. brushes, and planks for scrubbing suntans. There were also several folding ironing boards available. My monthly pay was substantially diminished by deductions for GI insurance and an allotment to my wife, resulting in very limited cash on hand on payday. One small way in which I was able to save a few dollars was to do my own laundry. To my recollection, it cost $1.80 per month to have your laundry processed at the post facility. It was washed, ironed, and neatly bundled if you contracted to have it done, and I envied those who did so. With the laundry equipment so convenient within the barracks, it took no heroic effort to maintain my appearance up to the colonel's requirements.

One morning after inspection the sergeant singled me out to report to the orderly room. Such orders were always a bit traumatic in spite of a clear conscience. It turned out I had been selected from the hundred or so men to pose for what I later learned was to be a poster. The photographer had his camera mounted on a tripod along with lighting and other paraphernalia, and I assumed as many poses as he requested. I guess in a way I was flattered since there were plenty of nice looking young men in the outfit, but an order was an order regardless of the military mindset behind it. There was also a nice looking young W.A.C. who arrived to pose both individually and jointly with me in several photos. I never learned more about the incident and soon dismissed it from my mind. If any of the photos every showed up in print anywhere it is unbeknownst to me. I assume it became just another scrapped idea.

I recall another incident where the press photographed me as I stood at attention at the White House while opening the car door for General Omar

Bradley to alight. A mishap occurred and the photo was never published in any newspaper that I could find, but it must exist in an archive somewhere. As I stated, I did my own laundry to save money. The $1.80 per month was sorely needed to support my wife and child. Every night I'd use a cake of yellow laundry soap and my G.I. brush to scrub my shirt, carefully removing all traces of perspiration. I'd hang the shirt in the barracks and by morning it would be dry. In the morning, I'd iron the shirt until it was crisp. The summer Class A uniform consisted of chino suntans. These tended to bleach out lighter after repeated laundering and subsequently became more easily soiled. To get old suntans thoroughly cleaned took a lot of scrubbing on the scrub plank with a G.I. brush and the strong yellow laundry soap. All this barracks laundering contributed to weakening the cloth a bit sooner than the periodic salvage day when uniforms were replaced by new issue. Needless to say, my blouse was getting a bit threadbare when I was called to drive General Bradley.

As I delivered General Bradley to the White House the press crowded around the limousine. As always, I exited and opened the door for him. At the very moment he stepped out of the limousine, I gave him my most rigid military salute and cameras went off from every direction. At the exact same moment, my elbow burst through my clean and neatly ironed, but weakened, shirtsleeve! This must have been an embarrassment for the army. A few days later, I was issued new shirts, so someone must have notified my commanding officer who arranged for a replacement uniform. The incident was never mentioned to me, however, and I never heard any repercussions. I never saw any published photo showing my elbow poking out through the tear in my sleeve.

Eventually my pay scale was increased, and I reached a level of solvency where I could have my laundry processed at the post facility at Fort Myer. My only complaint with their otherwise excellent service was the starch they put in the collar aggravated my neck, and the collar was required to be buttoned at all times.

Cpl. Richard Nabbe – 32920618
514ᵗʰ Ord. H.M. Co.
A.P.O. 230, %P.M. N.Y.C.

Pfc. Robert Nabbe
Motor Center Det.
2525ᵗʰ Service Unit
So. Post, Vt. Meyer,
Virginia

[Robert's address is crossed out on the envelope and handwritten is Forward to Station Hosp. Ward 2 Ft. Myer, Va]

Germany

April 13, 1945

Dear Rob,

Salutations from the dear old Hienie country. I received two letters from you last night and so I'm jotting down a few lines in return.

In reference to a letter I received from you concerning Mildred and I, you probably know she said "yes" and I intend to get engaged. However, I took a lot of things into careful consideration, and an awful lot of those things I did consider, was enclosed in the most helpful advice you forwarded to me. I appreciate to no extent the consideration you have extended to me, as far as advice goes, and also the understanding you have of my problem. I'll always accept any advice you have to offer and use it to its best advantage, so as I have said, time and again, please don't hesitate to do so. I don't intend to get married as soon as I get home Rob. I have a great deal of readjusting to do, and as you said previously, I have to find out which way the wind blows. I'm not a knot head as far as this all goes, so you can rely on me to do things in a sensible manner. Many thanks again for your helpful hand Rob. You can rest assured that it does help a great deal. You know Mickey writes me a letter every day, so you can see it keeps us fairly well contacted. She does a magnificent job at it and I often wonder how I got along this far without her. You made a real statement when you said there aren't many nice girls left. After I had been around the loop for awhile, I sure found that out. That for me, made me realize just what I had passed by.

I'm glad Margy likes those little shoes, I realize its no work of art, but if it pleases her a little, that enough thanks for me.

You can forget about that contact paper Rob. I picked some up in Paris. Thanks for all the effort though. I got a letter from Lorraine and it surprised the hell out of me. She's a swell sport and I bet she's really nice to know in person too. Say hello to her for me if you should see her.

I see you received the letter asking for "T" shirts, well I can sure use them all right. I guess I should thank you for that too. You do so darned much for me that all I say is "thanks". You're really swell Rob, believe me, and maybe you think it's not stapled in my rusty heart.

To-day we heard the president died. Quite a tragedy, but that's life itself. It's a shame he couldn't have seen the war end. I know how he would have wanted to.[88] The war is still going strong here and I suspect it won't be much longer now. I've got my fingers crossed anyway.

Well Rob that's all for to-day, I'm afraid. Give my love to all, and thanks again,
    Yer bruther
    Richie

---

88   President Franklin Delano Roosevelt died the previous day at his home in Warm Springs, Georgia. He suffered a cerebral hemorrhage. Roosevelt had been in failing health. Upon his death, Vice President Harry S. Truman assumed the presidency. Offering his consolation to the widowed Eleanor Roosevelt, Harry S. Truman asked, "Is there anything I can do for you?" Mrs. Roosevelt responded, "Is there anything we can do for you? For you are the one in trouble now." Sadly, Roosevelt did not live to see Germany surrender on May 8, 1945.

Cpl. Richard Nabbe – 32920618
514th ORD. CO. H.M.
A.P.O. 230 %P.M. N.Y.C.

Pfc. Robert Nabbe
Station Hospital
Ft. Meyer
Virginia

[The address is crossed out and handwritten is a forwarding address, Motor Center Det. Hq. MD, S. Post Ft. Myer, Va]
Germany

April 25, 1945

Dear Rob,

Say bud, are you trying to scare me out of my G.I. skivvies? When I saw that "General Hospital" on your envelope. My gosh, that's the last thing I ever thought you would have - appendicitis.[89] If it was your bladder turning rainbow colors from excess alcoholism, I wouldn't say anything.[90] Seriously though, I hope and pray that you are all right Rob. My gosh, you don't know how I worry over things like that. You should feel lucky that it was caught in time. Oh me! Everything happens to you! Let's get well real quick, please let me know how you are doing via paper and pen.

I got a cute V-mail from Joe U. It's of "Bugs Bunny" down where Joey is. Easter Greetings!!

Life here is very monotonous and uneventful. Outside of a Hienie ammo dump that the Americans burned and considerable oil dumps it's very peaceful. Oh, you should have seen that ammo dump blow. For two hours there was shells flying and exploding

---

89 Robert suffered a ruptured appendix because when he showed up for sick call, the officer on duty thought he was malingering and sent him back to work. By the time Robert was operated on, his appendix had burst. In addition, the anesthesia administered—ether—was ineffective, and Robert felt the entire operation. His protests were ignored, as the doctors did not believe he could feel any pain.

90 Richard again comments about drinking, a theme throughout all of the letters. The Nabbe men all enjoyed a nip or two, particularly beer. Robert and Richard's father, Fred, made beer during Prohibition.

all over the joint. I never heard such a racket in my life. More like all the past fourth of Julys rolled up into one. A very expensive fire, believe me. (Not for us though) We have a great big map of Germany and we have it all marked up with pins. Well according to my map, which is pretty accurate, there isn't much left for us to take over here anymore. Holy Cow, I don't see how those Hienies can keep on fighting. You should see what's left of their big factories, there isn't enough left to produce straight pins. Still they continue to fight on. I can't in any possible way see how they can last much longer. You'll see, in about a week, we'd have the whole country cut into pockets, and then it will be a process of elimination. It's a terrific mess here Rob and I don't think the Germans will do much fighting after this war. Believe it or not these bastards here (everybody included) are as arrogant as ever and I sincerely believe that this war won't keep them down. As soon as they get a chance, they'll start all over again. What we should do is shoot every bastard over here. Women, kids and all. You should see these girls here, some are so beautiful, blond and innocent looking. They smile at you and look like angels. No kidding Rob, you could fall for any of them, just like that. You say to yourself "Now how could a sweet young thing like that do any harm to anyone"? Well that sweet young thing is probably aching to slip a knife in your ribs, or plug you full of nice round holes. I guess it's hard to believe isn't it? Well you just take a dose of poison in the shape of a nice piece of candy and I'm sure you'll believe it quick. Not one of them is a goddamned bit good, and if I was told to shoot 'em all, I'd do it but quickly. They are worse than Japs, cause they are supposed to be civilized, but they just aren't human.[91] Now is your hair on end, are you below the mattress, is your heart where your toe nails are hung? Tune in next week and I'll tell you some more little useful facts about our poor abused German people. Till then Rob, take good care of yourself for me.

Your Bud
Richie

---

91   Richard says the Germans "are worse than Japs, cause they are supposed to be civilized." Most Americans were of European descent, with many families originally emanating from Germany. In spite of Richard's expressed hatred for the Germans, he still feels a kinship to them, unlike how he feels about the Japanese. Many Americans feared and loathed the Japanese partly because they were different. As Asians, they did not look like Europeans, and their customs and culture were vastly different. It is easy to demonize that which one does not know or understand. By this time, Richard is clearly war weary.

SURGERY IN THE ARMY

In April 1945, I took ill. I was working nights in the old White House Garage on C Street. I came off of night duty and had my breakfast. We had French toast, and I had a leaden stomach from it accompanied by severe pains. I thought I had indigestion. I went over to the PX and bought a bottle of Pepto Bismol and took it, but it didn't alleviate the problem. The next morning I was worse. Eventually I learned that I had a case of appendicitis. I was put in the hospital over at Fort Myer where an emergency appendectomy was performed.

An appendectomy today is like having a tooth out. But back in those days—fifty some years ago—it was a more serious operation. I particularly remember that they gave me a spinal. The pain was so intense that I was happy to have anything to kill it. As they started to cut me, however, I could feel the knife slicing in my abdomen. I'll tell you what; it really hurt. I bellowed out. The doctor said I shouldn't feel anything and I said, "Well, I do." He told me it wasn't possible. What followed was more chopping and more bellowing— and I did bellow! I am embarrassed to say I bellowed, but it was intensely painful. I said to the doctor, "I can move my toes," and I did. I showed him that I could move my toes to prove that the spinal hadn't taken after all. He was operating on me without anesthetic, so to speak. I went into shock. Someone quickly shoved an oxygen mask over my face. I started to throw up and the oxygen mask filled with vomit. I tried to push the mask off my face in order to breathe. The doctor thought I was fighting so he pushed the mask all the harder. Finally, I managed to get my fingers up underneath it enough for some matter to run out. Eventually the doctor saw what was happening. I heard him say, "We're losing him. His pulse is gone. His respiration is going." I was in deep shock and I said to myself, "What a hell of a way to die. Here I am in a non-combat position and I'm going to die in the army anyhow. " That was my only thought. It was pretty ironic.

In the end I recovered from the operation okay. I was in an old hospital that was part of Fort Myer, formerly a Civil War post. The hospital had housed Union soldiers that were recuperating at the end of the Civil War. Underneath the stairwell the soldiers had inscribed their names in the stairs. It was pretty interesting, that old hospital. It was a modern enough facility. There was no problem with the medical treatment. The attention I received was good.

Cpl. Richard Nabbe – 32920618
514th ORD. CO. H.M.
A.P.O. 230 %P.M. N.Y.C.

Pfc. Robert Nabbe
 32598454
Station Hospital
Ft. Meyer
Virginia

[Address on the envelope is crossed out and a forwarding address is handwritten: Motor Center Det. Hq. MD 2525 SCU, S. Post Ft. Myer VA.]

V-E Day – Germany[92]

May 9, 1945

Dear Rob,

Greeting from the conquerors old boy. Yes, its here Rob. The day we have all waited for so long has arrived. Now all we have to do is slap the hell out of Japan, and we can settle down for another peaceful existence for twenty years. Your brudder got drunk as a flat top in a hurricane. I drank everything that contained alcohol I could summon. Of course you realize I can't eat anything because my intestines have a bowline in 'em and food is rather repulsing. I never saw so many plastered GI's in all my born days. Maybe you think they don't deserve it. It's nearly a year now that we have been working merely seven days a week, plus I don't know how many hours a day. They were good to us though, they gave us the whole day off, so we could get rid of our hangovers. They realized we couldn't work anyway, so they killed two boids[93] with one 50 caliber machine gun. We gave up throwing rocks a long time ago. Well the vacation is over, so back to work we go. Of course you realize now that the war is over, we'll cut down on the hours we work. Probably be 12 or something like that. We only have all this equipment to clean,

---

92   VE Day was actually May 8, 1945. As Richard says, only part of the war was ended; there was still Japan to conquer, which the Allies did in August, 1945.

93   As is common throughout his letters, Richard uses dialect as a comedic device— "boids" for birds.

cosmoline[94] and etc., before we go anywhere. "There's always Japan yet", is the popular cry.[95] Boy I'm sure glad we aren't fighting three countries. I'd die of old age at that rate. Well give me a couple days home and they can ship me to Alaska. I don't care. Now is the question, will I get home? Probably not, but I can dream.[96]

Well how is the hem stitching these days? Do you feel pretty good? Are the stitches fancy or are they sloppy as ever? Mom said you were home for a day, so I guess I can dye my grey hair brown again. Take is easy, Rob or your incision might open up and your guts will all fall out. Be kind of clumsy carrying them around in your pocket. Seriously though, take it easy Rob. I hear you had a reunion down at the shore.[97] Oh, how I wish I could have been there. Well who knows, maybe I shall soon. Won't that be something! I realize they took your beer away for awhile old boy, but you should be happy cause now that your appendix is gone, you have all the more room to stow more beer. I wouldn't be surprised if the doc got squirted in the eye with the foam when he stuck you with that knife.

That's all for now Rob, take care. Give my regards to Marge and Suzie and I'll be seeing ya (I hope)

Yer Bruther
Richie

---

94   Cosmoline is a heavy grease-base preservative that is applied to all firearms to prevent rusting in shipping.

95   Even though war has ended in Europe, Richard isn't convinced that he is out of the woods knowing he could be shipped to the Pacific to fight the Japanese.

96   Richard dreams of going home, but he has to have enough points. He does stay in Germany for several more months, but by the end of the year is back home in Irvington, New Jersey.

97   The "shore" is the New Jersey Shore.

Cpl. Richard Nabbe – 32920618
514th ORD. CO. H.M.
A.P.O. 230 %P.M. N.Y.C.

Pfc. Robert Nabbe
32598454
Station Hospital
Ft. Meyer
Virginia

[Robert's address on the envelope is crossed out and handwritten is a forwarding address: Mtr. Cr. Det Hq. W. D 5/26/45.]

Germany

May 15, 1945

Dear Rob,

Received your letter today, so I shall answer it right now. It looks as though the boys where you are at are giving you the old one, two. You'll be back flat on your back before you know it, so cheer up lad, it can't go on forever. I know what you are going through, cause I had seven months of it myself. Of course, the conditions weren't the same, but I know what it's like and you have my deepest sympathy. The funny part about it was that I felt worse at the end of the seven months than I did when I started. It looks like it's going to start all over again too, now that the war's half over.

Speaking of the war, I know you think it's pretty sad when a guy gets fully disgusted over here. Well I've just past two years of this army life, and it won't be long before I'll be tacking three overseas stripes on my sleeve. Yep, a year and a half. I know it isn't much, but despite the fact that I'm just a rookie at this game (that's compared to some), I still don't care for it one damned bit. Sure you get lonesome, even with ten million people you get lonesome. It's only that at sometimes you get worse than others and it gets you down. I know I'll get home some day. When, I don't know, but in the meantime you just keep wasting time day after day, week after week, etc. Just cause the army says so. Christ I never wasted so much time in all my life as I have since I swapped those raggedy old civilian clothes for these lowly khakis. Well the war here is over, so now we go down to the Pacific for another year or maybe two. That doesn't help much as far *as the future goes does it? Mind you, I never expected to get discouraged when this war ended, no I just figured we might get home for a day or two before we took off again. That doesn't sound like an awful lot to ask, but actually it is. Considering the expense and time and a million other things involved. So it's a lot easier for the army to just float us on down to China and take on from there. In other words, it's just the same as ever, only we fight Japs instead of Hienies. (I don't know which is worse <u>yet</u>!) So I shall cease this foolish griping and just do as I always do and go where I'm sent. Doesn't do much good to do otherwise anyway. I haven't any where near enough points for a discharge, so that's out.[98] On with the war!! Meanwhile, we'll revert to a semi-garrison life, all chicken shit, but no garrison. It's started already and gets better as the days go by. Well that's the Army all over, so we accept that as only natural. I explained previously that I didn't intend to jump off the gang plank and get married.[99] On the contrary, it would certainly be foolish to get hitched on practically nothing. I'm sure that we'll be quite practical about the situation, and I'm certain all will come out fine. I'm trying to send what I can of my pay home each month, which should help a little bit. In fact, I should be a millionaire by the time I do get there.*

Well Rob, that's all for now. I'll see if I can't get you some of these morale crushers along more often, if I can. In the meantime, take care of yourself, and give my best to Marge and Suzy.

Your brother
Richie

---

98 Richard explains that he does not have enough points to get out of the army according to this points chart:

Advanced Service Rating Score

Points were awarded for the following

+1 points	Each month of service (between 16 Sept 1940-12 May 1945)
+1 points	Each month of service overseas (between 16 Sept 1940-12 May 1945)
+5 points	For the first and each ward received: DSC, LM, SS, DFC, SM, BS, AM, PH
+5 points	Campaign stars worn on theater ribbons
+12 points	Each child under 18 up to a limit of 3 children

99 While he states that he doesn't "intend to jump of the gang plank and get married," Richard did get married soon after returning home.

OBSERVATIONS: THE ROOSEVELTS AND SEGREGATION

In all my comings and goings I never once saw our president during my military service in Washington, D.C. Even though I was briefly stationed at the White House and even sat in his chair in his den, our paths never crossed. I did, however, have an occasion to converse with Mrs. Roosevelt, but not in the White House. One evening I was visiting the U.S.O. located quite close to the White House near Lafayette Square when Mrs. Roosevelt happened to drop in. For whatever reason she approached me and started a conversation that broached the subject of integration. This was an area close to her heart and she worked toward that end in many social ways. Approaching young white servicemen to encourage their acceptance of blacks was a good place from which to begin. At that time the military was still segregated and the black and white civilian communities were also distantly apart in the very southern-minded city of Washington.

The black population was employed in many more government functions than usual because of the induction of most white males into the military. Because of better paying employment and broader exposure and movement within the city, the black community anticipated a long deferred and overdue acceptance. Some areas in the black section became restless and vocal to a point where the military feared an uprising. All of Washington was a Military District and under full military control. Because of this in my first months in South Post Fort Myer each unit had one evening a week where we were confined to our barracks on "stand by" riot duty. Trucks and other military equipment were parked on the company street rather than in the Motor Pool on our "stand-by" tour that took place each Wednesday. The North Post of Fort Myer also headquartered the Military Police unit so adequate troops were available if the need arose. Fortunately the anticipated uprisings never materialized and in time the "stand by" status was cancelled. Segregation continued as before as old customs and habits die very slowly.

The one area of the military that was not segregated in Fort Myer was the post hospital. When I came to after my surgery, I was in the recovery room along side a black soldier whose name I later learned was Roosevelt. This was a fairly common name in the black community honoring our then president. The very same day an announcement came of the public address system that President Roosevelt had just died. The Black soldier lying in the next bed heard his name announced. He immediately bellowed out, "I ain't dead! I ain't dead!" In his awakening from the anesthesia he thought they were talking about him. Later on in our recovery I wrote some pretty steamy love letters for his lady friend that he dictated to me. Private Roosevelt was illiterate.

There were very few non-white officers in the army early on in the war. However, I was assigned on a number of occasions to chauffeur General Benjamin O. Davis who was a distinguished Black officer of high rank. He was a career soldier and a dignified genteel man that I enjoyed driving. He always addressed and spoke to me in the friendly courteous way as other generals I had known who came up slowly through the peacetime ranks. They always interacted positively with their subordinates.

Most of my fellow soldiers were from Georgia, Alabama, and other Deep South states that had an inherent disregard for people of color. I was one of the few Yankees in the outfit who didn't share their racial views. Perhaps that was one reason I was usually assigned to General Davis. During the war there was a sharp division between the races that was obvious in attitude and behavior on the part of the whites both in and out of the military.

There was a dark-skinned soldier of Indian lineage who was assigned to our outfit. The man was nearly black in color and the Southern boys almost rioted over the situation. The fact that the soldier was not African made no difference, and he was constantly referred to as "nigger." The chap was very well-educated and refined and affable, but ultimately he was re-assigned elsewhere to forestall the physical harm he would have experienced eventually.

I recently saw on television where retired General Benjamin Davis was awarded a long-deferred fourth star. I think this was the son of the General Davis I chauffeured, as he was an air force officer rather than in the U.S. Army. We have come a long way in our race relations since World War II, but I suspect we still have a bit of a way to go.

THE EXCITEMENT FADES

By this time, the war was well-organized. It wasn't over by a long shot, but it was fairly well-organized. There wasn't quite the intensity, the fervor or the urgency that I first experienced when the war began. My job simmered down to half of the volume of the traffic that I had handled before. The general officers were more or less dispersed all over the world by then. There weren't as many of them in the Pentagon so I really laid back. I didn't have heavy duty for quite a while. I was in and out but not with the same long times of driving as I had had before.

Form 75
MEDICAL DEPARTMENT, U. S. ARMY
(Revised April 11, 1936)

PATIENT'S PROPERTY CARD

Hospital _Fort Myer, Va._

Date _4-15-45_, 19___

Name _Nobbe_

Rank _______ Co. _______ Organization _______

NAME OF ARTICLE	NO. OF EACH	WHERE STORED (Tag No., Locker No., Envelope, etc.)
Belts		
Blankets		
Breeches, khaki		
Breeches, o. d	1	
Caps	1	
Coats, dress		
Coats, khaki		
Coats, o. d		
Collars		
Drawers	1	
Leggings		
Letters, U. S		
Marksman's badge		
Ornaments, cap		
Ornaments, collar		
Overcoats		
Shirts, civilian		
Shirts, o. d	1	
Shirts, white		
Shoes	1	
Suit case		

(OVER) 16—0123

NAME OF ARTICLE (Continued)	NO. OF EACH	WHERE STORED (Tag No., Locker No., Envelope, etc.)
Suit, civilian		
Suspenders		
Trousers, dress		
Trunk		
Trunk locker		
Undershirts	1	
T.1.R.	1	

The articles enumerated hereon were turned in by me on the date and at the place indicated.

____
Name of patient.

NOTE.—This card will be prepared in duplicate for each patient in hospital, as soon as possible after admission. It will be signed by the patient. The original will then be deposited in the proper files of the hospital, and the duplicate will be held by patient or kept at his bedside. (See AR 40-590.)

16—9123

REFLECTIONS ON MEDICAL SITUATIONS

On one of my immunization forms I noticed a date of 11-26-45 for a flu shot. This brought to mind an incident that was quite eventful. It was after I was administered the vaccine that I learned it was one that had been recently developed. There were about two hundred men in our outfit, and we were all inoculated at the same time. A day later there were one hundred and ninety-seven very sick GIs unable to fall out for morning roll call. There were only three soldiers able to report for duty. I was one of them. This caused a huge gap for drivers that fortunately the W.A.C. contingent was able to help fill. The war didn't stop because of a faulty serum. I thought at the time how beneficial it would have been if we could have sent the vaccine to the German Army. In a brief time everyone recovered but it sure was odd to see so many men attempting to stagger out of their bunks when the early morning whistle blew.

On another medical related incident I was posted on guard duty at the post gym when it was placed in use for giving the W.A.C.s their periodic physicals. The gymnasium was a holdover from the days when South Post Fort Myer was an officers' training station. Any physical exercises for the troop were held on the parade ground or the company streets so the gym found a reasonable use after all. The gymnasium can be seen as the large structure with a rounded roof in one of the photos of the campground. I remember the medical officer quite well as we had gotten to be casual friends during my service at Ft. Myer. He was a major by the name of Belgorod and not of the regular army persuasion. I asked him how he enjoyed doing all those examinations on the young women, and he replied that he would trade places with me guarding the door if I would give him the gun. I guess he would rather have dealt with a bunch of whiney gold bricking men. It was always a challenge to chase away the GIs trying to peek in at the disrobed ladies, and while I had a weapon, I didn't think it reasonable to draw it on a bunch of red-blooded curious males doing what comes naturally.

Sanitation was an absolute must in the army, and while the officers and non-coms enforced the official military requisites, it was surprising how effectively the ordinary G.I. handled situations not in the manual. We had one backwoods type whose personal hygiene was in absentia. He always smelled from the feet up. Under field or combat conditions it would have been different, but in the elite outfit that it was our good fortune to be in, it was intolerable. We were issued extra uniforms and clothing in order to maintain a sharp appearance and bathing facilities were plentiful. There were no excuses for going around reeking. I do recall this chap was detailed as a motorcycle courier and in retrospect understand his assigned duty out in the open air. It was the consensus that our non-conformer—after repeated hints to shower—needed a G.I. bath courtesy of the troops. This is a harsh but effective procedure and one in which one session usually suffices. The men forcibly removed the offender's clothing and scrubbed him down on the shower floor with yellow soap and G.I. brushes. This left his hide red but odor free for the first time in weeks. While he continued to look like a slob, at least we could get downwind from him until he was transferred out shortly thereafter.

Following pages: Private Nabbe's immunization record (front) and (back)

IMMUNIZATION REGISTER

Mc

LAST NAME	FIRST NAME	ASN
NABBE,	ROBERT	32598454

MTR-STR

GRADE	CO.	REGT.	AGE	RACE
PVT. PFC	H		9-12-1919	W

SMALLPOX VACCINE

DATE	TYPE OF REACT	MED. OF.
DEC 17 1942		

TRIPLE TYPHOID VACCINE

DATES OF ADMIN.		MED. OF
SERIES	1st 2d 3d	
1st	DEC 1 1942 12-30-42 SEP 2 1944 PC	
2d	1-6-43 SAB.	
3d	sec 9-30-43 SAB	

TETANUS TOXOID

INIT. VACC.		STIM. DOSES	
DATE	MED. OF.	DATE	MED.OF.
1st	7-12-93	Stim 9-30-43 SM
2d	6-43	SAB.
3d	5-3-43	SAB

YELLOW FEVER VACCINE

DATE	LOT NO.	AMOUNT	MED. OF.

OTHER VACCINE

SEASES	DATE	TYPE	DOSES	MED.OF.
TYPE	O			DAB

2 Maj. Sgt Belford M.C.

IMMUNIZATION REGISTER
AND OTHER MEDICAL DATA
(SEE AR 40-210)

M C

NAME (LAST, FIRST, MID. INITIAL)	ASN
Nabbe, Robert	32598454

DATE OF BIRTH	RACE	BLOOD GROUP	MED. OFF.
9-12-1910	W	O	SHB

SMALLPOX VACCINE

DATE	TYPE OF REACTION	MED. OFF.
12-17-42		HM
JUL 1 9 1945	Vaccinoid	NO

TRIPLE TYPHOID VACCINE		TYPHUS VACCINE	
DATES EACH DOSE	MED. OFF.	DATES EACH DOSE	MED. OFF.
12-17-42			
12-30-42			
1-6-43	SHB		
9-30-43	SHB		
9-2-44	HO		
JUL 1 9 1945	NO		

TETANUS TOXOID		CHOLERA VACCINE	
DATES EACH DOSE	MED. OFF.	DATES EACH DOSE	MED. OFF.
12-17-42			
1-6-43	SHB		
4-12-43	SHB		
5-3-43	SHB		
9-30-43	SHB		

YELLOW FEVER VACCINE

DATE	LOT NO.	MED. OFF.

W. D., A. G. O. FORM 8-117 15 AUGUST 1944

THIS FORM SUPERSEDES M. D. FORM 81, 23 SEPTEMBER 1942, WHICH WILL NOT BE USED AFTER RECEIPT OF THIS REVISION.

16—42404-1

FT. MYER, VIRGINIA BARRACKS
IN DISTANCE 1944

TRANSPORTING THE DEAD

Before I had the problem over in the C Street Barracks in Washington, and while I was still out in the Ft. Myer-Pentagon complex, I was assigned to burial detail. The kids who were coming back in caskets were being buried in Arlington. Because of my proximity to Arlington National Cemetery and because I was not as busy driving general officers as I had been, I was assigned to this duty.

It was the saddest of all duties. I would go to the train stations and pick up the families of the soldiers being interred. I was at the family's disposal with the vehicle until the funeral was over. I took the families to the services, to their hotel, back and forth to the cemetery—whatever was required. The government was most gracious in extending to the families of the deceased this courtesy. I used to have to attend all the interments. Seeing parents, young wives, sisters, and brothers all broken up was difficult. The face of war came home here in our backyard, particularly the aftermath of war.

DRIVING THE WOUNDED

When I was driving the ambulance I would go meet aircraft at National Airport. In the later stages of the war, the army was field treating the injured soldiers and then bringing them to the states by aircraft for complete reconstructive treatment. I would go and pick up these cases and take them to Walter Reed Hospital where they were admitted for whatever repairs were necessary.

One of the things that I recall so vividly was the prosthesis room where all of these kids were sitting around waiting to be fitted with arms or legs. I saw kids who were blinded. They were all kids, young kids. It was very saddening to see. This war was a heck of a way to settle a political dispute. It affected a lot of people for the rest of their lives. Those who were buried early on didn't know anymore about it, but those who lived without their arms or legs spent the entire rest of their lives suffering the effects of war.

I was so fortunate never to have to go into battle. I still think of my brother who was never quite the same after he came back from the war because he experienced a lot of combat and trauma. A happy-go-lucky kid came back a bitter person and he remained so for the rest of his life.

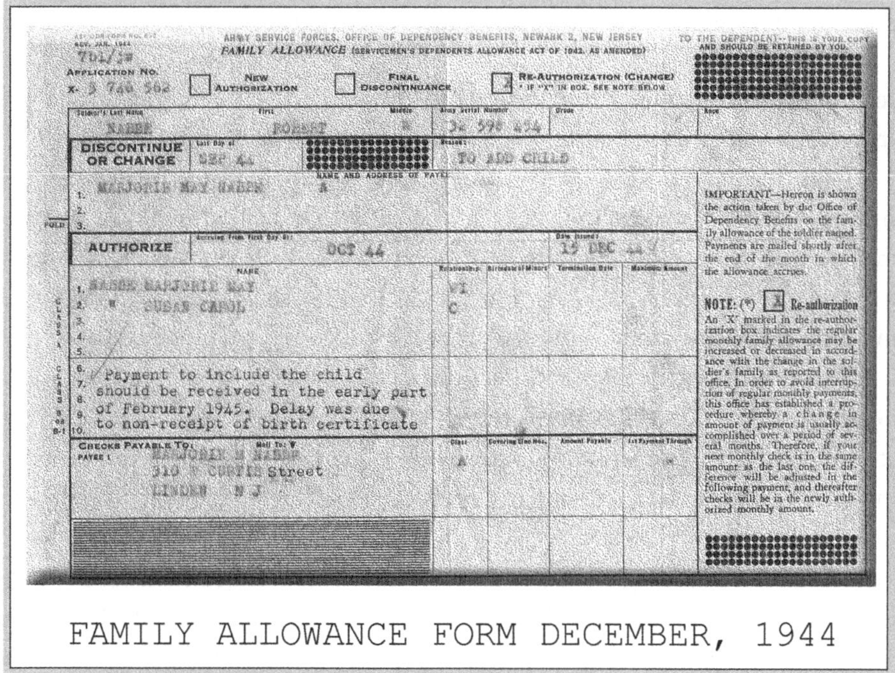

FAMILY ALLOWANCE FORM DECEMBER, 1944

THE WAR WINDS DOWN

There were so many times when I just had no idea how long the war was going to continue. Even though I knew we were making gains in the different theaters of operation, there was no way of telling how much more service would be required of an individual. I know that a year went by and a second year went by and then a third. I said to myself, "Will I ever get out of this army?" I wasn't aware that in just a few more months I would be released.

I can recall an exceptionally memorable moment. I was in the barracks, and the barracks were quite empty. One the sergeants came along and said that we had dropped an atom bomb on Japan. Of course I didn't even know what an atom bomb was. I had a suspicion that it was a nuclear device, but at the time there wasn't anything that was even rumored as a possibility.

Strangely enough one of the generals I drove quite often was Leslie Groves who was in charge of the Manhattan Project that developed the atomic weapons. I never overheard one word spoken about the project in all the times I drove General Groves even though officers conversed freely with their aides in my presence.

After the bombing of Japan, I knew it was the beginning of the end. In my own small way with the limited awareness that I had of the overall picture I sensed that things were tapering down substantially. I did less and less driving, and there were fewer and fewer high staff officers that needed chauffeuring. I just had a comfortable feeling that we were getting closer to the end. I think the bomb probably triggered my thinking in that direction. It just seemed like the whole Pentagon, as enormous as it was and as complex and busy as it was, to be lessening in intensity. I guess that's about the best way to explain it.

About that time, I was promoted to corporal. The war was almost over, but I didn't realize it at that moment. My promotion was probably related to my driving General Eisenhower. I believe he had something to do with it. I do know that I received from General Eisenhower an autographed photograph that he wanted me to have.

Cpl. Richard Nabbe – 32920618
514ᵗʰ ord. H.M. Co.
A.P.O. 339, P.M.NYC.N.Y

Pfc. Robert Nabbe
Motor Center Detach
2525ᵗʰ Service Unit
So. Post. Ft. Meyer
Virginia

Kassel Germany

June 4, 1945

Dear Rob –

Egads and halitosis chum, but I was sure glad to hear from you. Now that I know you are all right again, I feel much more at ease. Mom told me you had a furlough and I'm glad you have enjoyed it as for writing to me, don't let it bother you. Once in a while is fine. I know what its like to try writing all the time and it's really quite difficult. The picture of Suzy is really cute. She's a beautiful baby and something to be very proud of. I've compared her to the other photos you sent and already she's grown quite a bit. She'll be all grown up before you know it. In return, I'm sending you one of my ugly puss that was taken here. You can tuck it away in some dark corner of your wallet where it won't embarrass you too much. However that's the way I look, so dots dot![100]

The point situation stinks as far as I'm concerned. I've got 54 now and if I get those other two battle stars, it will be 64. You see I've a long haul ahead. I've got three battle stars now officially and I anticipate getting two more. However, having no purple hearts (thank God) or congressional medals of honor, or a wife and three kids and I'm not over forty years of age, I have quite a haul ahead of me. Seriously, I don't believe I'll be home for a year or so. We don't get much encouragement as for as going home goes, so I've just given up and decided to let fate take its course.

I sure would like to go fishing again for just one time. We go fishing here too, but not with a hook and line. You just get about a dozen "frog" grenades and stroll down to the river. It's a guaranteed method even if it isn't sportsmanlike. The concussion stuns the fish and they come up to the top. All you do is rake 'em in. Simple, eh? One of these

---

100 "Dot's dot" is his way of saying, "That's that."

days one of those grenades will go off ahead of time and I'll go around sporting a well perforated chassis. That's called amusement. Arf! Arf!

I'm glad Mom got those flowers. I didn't think my letter would reach Dot in time. It's very little to offer, but it's a little bit. That's a real good way to spend money. In fact, there just isn't a better way.

I was an office clerk for quite awhile, but I quit that job and now I'm trying to get into the welding dept. I think I'd like that. That paper work is alright if you like that sort of stuff, but I just don't get along with it. Maybe I'll be better off this way.

Well Rob me boy, take it easy and don't bust your gut open again. I have a sweater going home that mom sent to me. I sure hope it gets there. Let me know if you hear anything about it will you? I also have a German mouser rifle[101] on the way too. It's all cosmolined and wrapped, so I guess it will be quite a job to clean up.

Say hello to Margie and Suzy for me and I'll let you know if anything develops.
Bye
Yer Brother
Richie

PS - Thanks for the insert of Lorraines letter. I just answered one she sent to me.

---

101 Robert has this to say about the German Mouser rifle: "I never saw Richard's Mouser war trophy and question whether it ever got home."

___ Richard Nabbe 32920618
___th Ord. Co. Heavy Maint.
A.P.O. 339 %P.M. N.Y.C.

Pfc. Robert Nabbe
Motor Center Detach
2525 Service Unit
So. Post, Ft. Meyer
Virginia

Kassel, Germany

June 20, 1945

Dear Rob,

Nice to hear you are well again and back to the old grind. Not nice to be back at the grind, but being well, I guess you understand. Your philosophy that you orated in your letter is quite true, but as I've been slightly educated during this little tour, I'll let you in on a secret. Wars will never end, so don't kid yourself, all that hot air they spill is purely, hot air. Right now, at this very moment, the conquered enemy is cooking up the next skirmish. Oh yes, they are beaten all right, but just for now. I'm not fooling Rob, this war is only a victory from a military standpoint. The poor beaten down German is just a coat of paint nothing more. You want to know a few more things I've learned? Well take a man as an individual, take him from his little circle that his life circulates around, and what is he? Nothing. Just another guy. How do I know that? Well take a look at this joint. We have thousands of people here of every nationality conceivable. Nobody likes anybody else. The Poles hate the Germans, the Russians don't like anybody either. The Germans prefer Americans cause they can get a lot more out of them. Outside of that, there's no love lost. Christ, what a mess. You have to walk the street with a carbine in one hand and a tommy gun in the other. Not because some body will shoot you cause they don't like you, but because maybe some jerk wants to try his gun out and needs a target. This sounds like a page from inner sanctum[102] doesn't it? Well maybe it is, but here the whole thing in a nutshell. Human life is the cheapest commodity over here. Dying is like a kissing a girl, here one minute, the next gone. Well

---

102 Inner Sanctum Mysteries, a popular old-time radio program that aired from January 7, 1941 to October 5, 1952, was created by producer Hyman Brown. A total of 526 episodes were broadcast.

*why is it that way? It's because most are better off dead, and they know it and don't
give a damn what happens from day to day. Nice girls (German) let some dirty Polack
paw all over them, or American too, for just that reason. Common prostitutes who were
really decent stuff not too long ago. Just hoisting their skirts for anything that they can
get. Some of these babes are as pretty as a picture, blonde and really beautiful. Some are
very highly educated and came from families that are all dead. That's one of the biggest
reasons that they go haywire, no folks, homes or anything. Just living from day to day,
that's all. So you see Rob, it doesn't take shells and bullets to drive a man nuts, a man
can endure an awful lot when it comes to things like that, but this is different, this is just
like everything is down to its lowest form of degradation. No hope, no future. It's a gods
awful pity and it can make you sicker than a rocking boat on a rough sea. So you see
that all this is more or less to sum up a point. I don't want any sympathy from anybody.
I don't deserve or want it. All I want to do is get the hell out of here before I forget just
what there is worth living for. This type of letter isn't at all like me Rob, but after all I
want you to know what we think over here. I miss you folks terribly and I do so want to
come home, but from the developments that have occurred here, I've adopted an attitude
of let the world roll by, and by and by I'll see you all again. Right now, it's no USA,
but eventually something is bound to happen, so I'll just wait and see. That's enough of
that cynical stuff, you probably can't get any sense from it any how. It's so difficult to
explain what one feels in a letter. The difficulty is that the person receiving it won't derive
the correct meaning. Ordinarily I'd tear this up, but I think I'll send it to you any-how.*

*I'll close here Rob, but I want you to know that I'm very happy and glad that you
weren't here all through this campaign. You did your part and probably a lot more
than you realize. Keep this thought in mind, chum, although your life at times seems
so monotonous and insignificant, you are way ahead of us all over here. You'll go home
eventually and you have a nice family started so you should be happy about that if
nothing else. Keep kicking Rob, and eventually everything will be all right again.*

Your brother,
Richie

PS Love to Marge and baby

Cpl. Richard Nabbe 32920618
3423rd Ord. M A __ Co.
A.P.O. 758, %P.M. N.Y.C.N.Y.

September 7, 1945

Dear Rob,

Just a few lines to let youze know I haven't forgotten you. I know now that Grandpa died and you did get home to go to the funeral. I'm sorry I didn't get a chance to be there myself, but you know how tis. I'm on the home stretch now kid, so <u>don't</u> send any Christmas packages to me. I hope to be barely hanging on to a bar with you on that joyful day. So, till then —

Richie

Bet you thought I'd forgotten.

DISCHARGE

My promotion to corporal came just prior to my discharge because I have in front of me a copy of a telegram that was sent to me as dated December 2, 1945. It shows me as PFC Robert Nabbe, Motor Center Detachment. It was a telegram from my sister, Dorothy. It said, "Richard's in states and well. Call tonight. Letter follows. Dot." Oh, to know that Richard was back in the states safe and sound was one of the bigger burdens to come off of my heart and mind. It was comforting to know that he was back safely. This was after the capitulation of the Axis forces and that's why I kept thinking, "Holy smokes, how much longer can I be kept in the service?"

Richard was ultimately discharged before me. He went in after I went in but he got out before I got out. I have Richard's discharge in front of me. He was released from the military on the seventh of December 1945, four years to the day after Pearl Harbor—a strange coincidence. Richard was sent home by ship, and surprisingly, as the ship crossed the Atlantic, it encountered a bad storm. The ship rolled onto its side, and Richard thought he wouldn't make it home after all. "I had gone through the hell of war only to see my life slipping away in a storm at sea," he explained. Eventually, though, the ship righted itself and weathered the storm. Had it not, everyone on board would have been lost. Even though Richard had survived the D-Day invasion and the Battle of the Bulge, it was one of the most frightening experiences of his life.

BROTHERS IN WAR, ROBERT AND
RICHARD NABBE, 1944

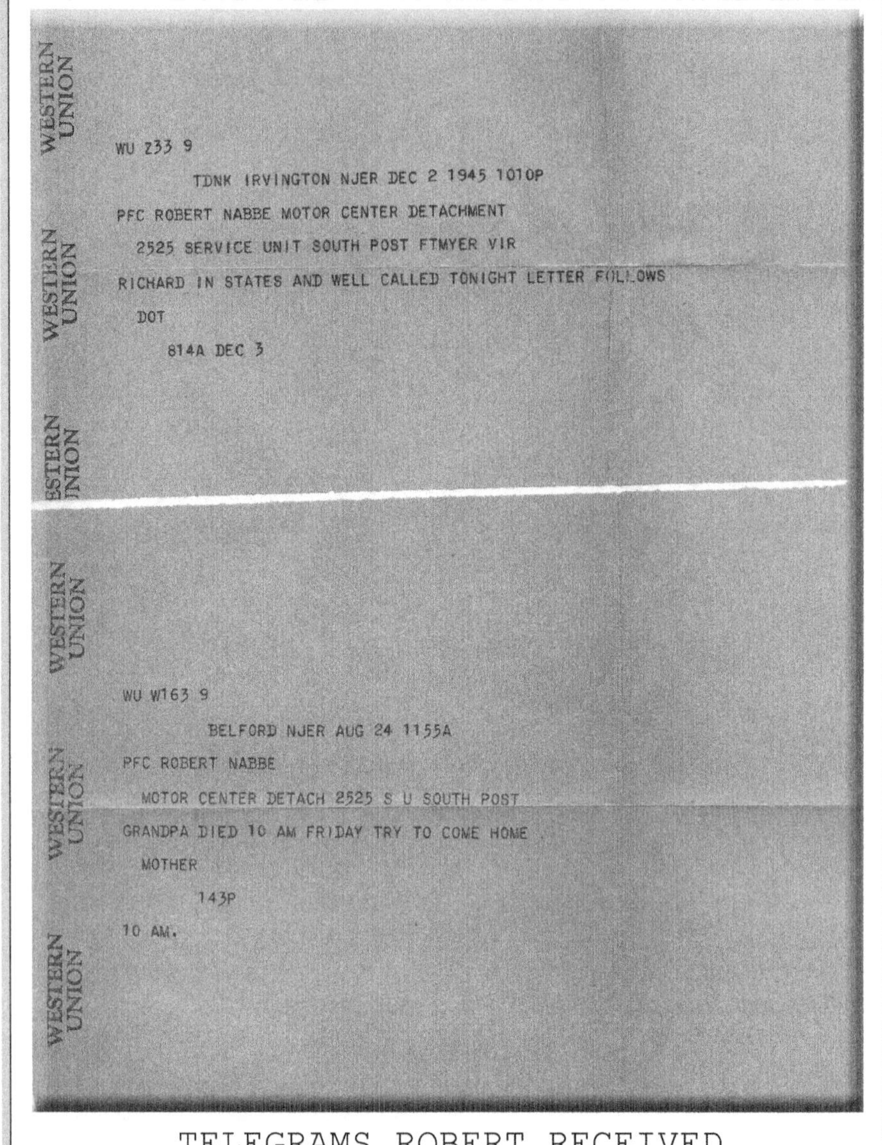

TELEGRAMS ROBERT RECEIVED
DURING THE WAR.

Army of the United States

SEPARATION QUALIFICATION RECORD

SAVE THIS FORM. IT WILL NOT BE REPLACED IF LOST

This record of job assignments and special training received in the Army is furnished to the soldier when he leaves the service. In its preparation, information is taken from available Army records and supplemented by personal interview. The information about civilian education and work experience is based on the individual's own statements. The veteran may present this document to former employers, prospective employers, representatives of schools or colleges, or use it in any other way that may prove beneficial to him.

1. LAST NAME—FIRST NAME—MIDDLE INITIAL			MILITARY OCCUPATIONAL ASSIGNMENTS		
NABBE, ROBERT W			10. MONTHS	11. GRADE	12. MILITARY OCCUPATIONAL SPECIALTY
2. ARMY SERIAL No.	3. GRADE	4. SOCIAL SECURITY No.	36	Tec 5	Chauffeur (345)
32 598 454	TEC 5	136-09-4698			
5. PERMANENT MAILING ADDRESS (Street, City, County, State)					
310 W Curtis St., Linden, Union Co., N.J.					
6. DATE OF ENTRY INTO ACTIVE SERVICE	7. DATE OF SEPARATION	8. DATE OF BIRTH			
17 Dec 42	11 Feb 46	12 Sept 19			
9. PLACE OF SEPARATION					
FORT DIX, NEW JERSEY					

SUMMARY OF MILITARY OCCUPATIONS

13. TITLE—DESCRIPTION—RELATED CIVILIAN OCCUPATION

CHAUFFEUR: Served with the Motor Center Detachment, War Department Motor Pool, Hq., Hq. Company, 2525 Service Command Unit as chauffeur.

Chauffeured general officers in the city of Washington, D.C. Was stationed at War Department motor pool, on call to chauffeur any general officers needing transportation.

WD AGO FORM 100
1 JUL 1945

This form supersedes WD AGO Form 100, 15 July 1944, which will not be used.

ENLISTED RECORD AND REPORT OF SEPARATION
HONORABLE DISCHARGE

1. LAST NAME - FIRST NAME - MIDDLE INITIAL	2. ARMY SERIAL NO.	3. GRADE	4. ARM OR SERVICE	5. COMPONENT
NABBE ROBERT W	32 598 454	TEC 5	TC	AUS

6. ORGANIZATION	7. DATE OF SEPARATION	8. PLACE OF SEPARATION
Mortor Center Det 2525th SU	11 Feb 46	SEP CTR FT DIX NJ

9. PERMANENT ADDRESS FOR MAILING PURPOSES	10. DATE OF BIRTH	11. PLACE OF BIRTH
310 W Curtis St Linden NJ	12 Sep 19	Newark NJ

12. ADDRESS FROM WHICH EMPLOYMENT WILL BE SOUGHT	13. COLOR EYES	14. COLOR HAIR	15. HEIGHT	16. WEIGHT	17. NO.DEPEND.
See 9	Hazel	Blond	5-8	178 LBS.	2

18. RACE	19. MARITAL STATUS	20. U.S. CITIZEN	21. CIVILIAN OCCUPATION AND NO.
WHITE W / NEGRO / OTHER (specify)	SINGLE / MARRIED X / OTHER (specify)	YES X / NO	Assembler Electrical Inst. 6-78.632

MILITARY HISTORY

22. DATE OF INDUCTION	23. DATE OF ENLISTMENT	24. DATE OF ENTRY INTO ACTIVE SERVICE	25. PLACE OF ENTRY INTO SERVICE
10 Dec 42		17 Dec 42	Newark NJ

SELECTIVE SERVICE DATA	26. REGISTERED: YES X / NO	27. LOCAL S.S.BOARD NO. 17	28. COUNTY AND STATE: Essex Co NJ	29. HOME ADDRESS AT TIME OF ENTRY INTO SERVICE: 241 Nesbit Terrace NJ

30. MILITARY OCCUPATIONAL SPECIALTY AND NO.	31. MILITARY QUALIFICATION AND DATE (i.e., infantry, aviation and marksmanship badges, etc.)
Chauffeur 345	None

32. BATTLES AND CAMPAIGNS

NONE

33. DECORATIONS AND CITATIONS

AMERICAN SERVICE MEDAL   GOOD CONDUCT MEDAL   WORLD WAR II VICTORY MEDAL

34. WOUNDS RECEIVED IN ACTION

NONE

35. LATEST IMMUNIZATION DATES				36. SERVICE OUTSIDE CONTINENTAL U.S. AND RETURN		
SMALLPOX	TYPHOID	TETANUS	OTHER (specify)	DATE OF DEPARTURE	DESTINATION	DATE OF ARRIVAL
17Dec42	30Sep43	3Sep45	None		NONE	

37. TOTAL LENGTH OF SERVICE						38. HIGHEST GRADE HELD
CONTINENTAL SERVICE			FOREIGN SERVICE			
YEARS	MONTHS	DAYS	YEARS	MONTHS	DAYS	
3	1	25	0	0	0	TEC 5

39. PRIOR SERVICE

NONE

40. REASON AND AUTHORITY FOR SEPARATION

CONV OF THE GOV'T AR 615-365 15DEC44 & RR1-1 DEM TWX WGL 37 500 WDGAP 15 Jan 46

41. SERVICE SCHOOLS ATTENDED	42. EDUCATION (Years)		
	Grammar	High School	College
NONE	8	4	0

PAY DATA

43. LONGEVITY FOR PAY PURPOSES			44. MUSTERING OUT PAY		45. SOLDIER DEPOSITS	46. TRAVEL PAY	47. TOTAL AMOUNT, NAME OF DISBURSING OFFICER
YEARS	MONTHS	DAYS	TOTAL	THIS PAYMENT			
3	2	2	$ 300	$100	None	$ 3.60	$104.01 J HARRIS COL FD

INSURANCE NOTICE

IMPORTANT   IF PREMIUM IS NOT PAID WHEN DUE OR WITHIN THIRTY-ONE DAYS THEREAFTER, INSURANCE WILL LAPSE. MAKE CHECKS OR MONEY ORDERS PAYABLE TO THE TREASURER OF THE U. S. AND FORWARD TO COLLECTIONS SUBDIVISION, VETERANS ADMINISTRATION, WASHINGTON 25, D.C.

48. KIND OF INSURANCE			49. HOW PAID		50. Effective Date of Allotment Discontinuance	51. Date of Next Premium Due (One month after 50)	52. PREMIUM DUE EACH MONTH	53. INTENTION OF VETERAN TO		
Nat. Serv.	U.S. Govt.	None	Allotment	Direct to V. A.				Continue	Continue Only	Discontinue
X				X	31 Jan 46	28 Feb 46	$6.60	X		

54.	55. REMARKS (This space for completion of above items or entry of other items specified in W. D. Directives)
[RIGHT THUMB PRINT]	LAPEL BUTTON ISSUED ASR SCORE 2 SEP 45-45 Certificate of Eligibility No. 2478 220 has been issued by the Veterans Administration to be used for the future request of any Guaranty or insurance benefit under Title III of the Serviceman's Readjustment Act of 1944, as amended, that may be available to the person to whom this separation paper was issued.

56. SIGNATURE OF PERSON BEING SEPARATED	57. PERSONNEL OFFICER (Type name, grade and organization - signature)
Robert W Nabbe	G W MILES CWO USA *G W Miles*

WD AGO FORM 53-55   This form supersedes all previous editions of
 1 November 1944   WD AGO Forms 53 and 55 for enlisted persons

MILITARY EDUCATION

14. NAME OR TYPE OF SCHOOL—COURSE OR CURRICULUM—DURATION—DESCRIPTION

NONE

CIVILIAN EDUCATION

15. HIGHEST GRADE COMPLETED	16. DEGREES OR DIPLOMAS	17. YEAR LEFT SCHOOL	OTHER TRAINING OR SCHOOLING	
4 yrs. H.S.	Diploma	1936	20. COURSE—NAME AND ADDRESS OF SCHOOL—DATE	21. DURATION

18. NAME AND ADDRESS OF LAST SCHOOL ATTENDED — NONE

Frank Morrell H.S., Irvington, N.J.

19. MAJOR COURSES OF STUDY

Academic

CIVILIAN OCCUPATIONS

22. TITLE—NAME AND ADDRESS OF EMPLOYER—INCLUSIVE DATES—DESCRIPTION

ASSEMBLER ELEC. INST. 6-78.632 for Weston Electrical Inst. Corp. Newark, N.J., from 1940 to 1942.

Assembled voltmeters, ammeters and other electrical instruments. Used hand electrician tools after complete assembly, calibrated and checked instrument for accuracy of performance. Followed sketches and blueprints, made minor repairs. Did all type of electric machine shop work.

ADDITIONAL INFORMATION

23. REMARKS

NONE

24. SIGNATURE OF PERSON BEING SEPARATED	25. SIGNATURE OF SEPARATION CLASSIFICATION OFFICER	26. NAME OF OFFICER (Typed or Stamped)
Robert W Nabbe	*G. W. Von Schlichten*	W W VON SCHLICHTEN MAJ AGD

U. S. GOVERNMENT PRINTING OFFICE—O-657477

THE OFFER OF A UNIQUE OPPORTUNITY

My military service had petered down to a maintenance level. One day I was called in to see the commanding officer. He offered me a promotion to master sergeant. Now that's a very, very tempting rank in the army. It is the highest grade of non-commissioned officer. It pays the most and keeps you as a serviceman with all the benefits. If you became a second lieutenant you hardly made nearly as much, and you had to pay for all your uniforms, meals, and everything else. So to be a master sergeant was a real coup. Anybody who can reach that level in the military and retire from it gets a terrific pension.

The Army wanted me to accompany a general to Russia as a driver. When it was offered to me, the commanding officer reminded me that I already had a hitch in. He said, "You're still a young fellow and before you know it, you'll have enough service time to retire. You'll still be a young man and you'll have a pension for the rest of your life as well as medical benefits. Your wife and daughter will be provided for." It sounded very enticing, but I told him that I wasn't a military-type person. I said I was a civilian soldier willing enough to support my country, but I did not want to make a career of it.

The same fellow that I mentioned earlier who also drove limousines took the job. When I turned it down, I mentioned it to him. He went in and requested it. The fellow was a single chap and didn't have a family. He wrote me quite a few letters from Russia. Russia was real torn, devastated after the war. He asked me for simple things like, shaving cream, razors, and Sunday newspapers. The chap loved to have a Sunday paper. I sent him all those things for a while. I gathered from his letters that the duty was less than a vacation because of the privations that the Russian nation was suffering. I was glad I hadn't accepted the position because I really didn't want to go. I wanted to go home to Margie and Susan.

SEPARATION

I ultimately went back to the garage to report for duty and they told me to go back to the barracks and pack my stuff. My separation had come through. That was February 11, 1946. I turned in everything and I went home first.

What were they going to do to me now even if I was a little A.W.O.L.? They weren't going to put me in jail anymore. I went home to see Margie and Sue. Then I got our car and drove back to Fort Dix where I went through the separation process.

THE ARMY RESERVES

The officer in charge of the separation formality asked me to sign up for the Army Reserves. He said that even though the war was over it was still everybody's patriotic duty to serve as a citizen soldier. I agreed. It involved one meeting each month at the National Guard Armory. Then, two weeks a year you had to go away to military camp. The government paid you for this. I would have accrued all kinds of military benefits. But at the last minute— you know it was one of those funny things where somebody puts a pen in your hand and you're just about ready to sign it and all of a sudden you have a second thought and lay the pen down. That's exactly the way it was. He handed me the pen, I started to sign, and I had an intuitive insight. I said, "No." As much I agreed that I should continue to be available to protect my country's interest, I didn't think I wanted to do sign up after all. I laid the pen down. So he just crumpled the form up and threw it in the basket.

Whatever inner voice was whispering in my ear, it certainly was the right one because the Korean War started not too long after. Had I been in the Army Reserves and the National Guard, I'd have marched off to that war, and maybe I wouldn't have been here to write this.

EPILOGUE

When Richard returned from the war, he brought with him many trophies that he acquired while in battle. These included pieces of Germany military uniforms—especially pins, belt buckles, and medals—the metal front piece of a German officer's cap, two officers' swords, and a red Nazi balustrade flag along with fliers signed by General Eisenhower that had been dropped from planes urging German soldiers to surrender while promising them safe keeping by Allied Forces. In addition, Richard mounted all the photos he took in Europe into a black photo album, which survives. Richard would never discuss how he obtained the artifacts and refused to talk about his war experiences. Prior to his death, Richard passed along these items to a family member, but on the condition that he did not have to discuss them nor would he answer any questions. Robert, too, kept mementos of his service as a chauffeur. These include the leather gloves he wore when chauffeuring General Eisenhower, and an autographed photo of Eisenhower sent to him by the general at war's end, and menus to Christmas banquets. Robert also retained his uniform and pieces of it remain in the family. Medals, campaign ribbons, marksmanship awards, and other mementos from both men also survive and are retained in the family archive.

After the war ended and Robert and Richard were discharged, their lives took different paths though they remained close their entire lives. Richard married his wartime girlfriend, Mildred (Mickey) Mrazak, but the union produced no children. They remained married until Mildred's death in the late 1980s. Soon after the war, funded by his mother-in-law, Richard purchased and ran a gas station in New Jersey, which he maintained for a couple of years. When that venture ended, he opened a machine shop using an industrial lathe to make metal parts for larger machinery. After he closed the machine shop, Richard assumed a position as a highly skilled tool and die maker, a position he had held prior to the war. He continued in this career for the remainder of his working life. In the early 1990s, Richard contracted brain cancer, and died in 1992.

As did many World War II servicemen, Robert availed himself of the GI Bill and attended Newark School of Fine and Industrial Arts, a highly rated art institution. After completing the three-year program, Robert graduated and received an award, a special acknowledgment of his senior project that wove together the story of the Morris Canal—which stretched from the Delaware River to the Raritan River—via a series of murals that were installed in the cafeteria of the YWCA in Newark, New Jersey. While attending art school, Robert worked nights as a mechanic in a gas station. Still living in the home of Marjorie's parents in Linden, Robert and Marjorie wanted to set out on their own and planned a move to Florida after a brief trip to evaluate the Sunshine State. In 1948, daughter Melissa was born, and in 1949 the family moved to St. Petersburg, Florida. Knowing he could not support his family as an itinerant artist, Robert went to work for Ace Neon Sign Company, first working as a designer and a salesman and later as a sheet metal mechanic. As a master craftsman, Robert excelled in this field. Daughter Robin was born in 1954 making the family complete. In 1960, Robert left Ace and traded workingman's clothes for a suit and tie. He went to work for First Federal Savings and Loan, first as a teller and later as a real estate appraiser. After a successful career in this realm, Robert retired from this position and relocated to Tennessee where, at age 95, he resides today.

CPSIA information can be obtained at www.ICGtesting.com
Printed in the USA
LVOW05s0231021214

416627LV00011B/130/P